RIPPED CLEAN

DOWN TO NOTHING BUT THE CROSS

Group

(†) simply youth ministry

Stripped Clean
Down to Nothing But the Cross

group.com
simplyyouthministry.com

Credits
Executive Developer: Patty Smith
Chief Creative Officer: Joani Schultz
Copy Editor: Nancy Friscia
Cover Art Director/Designer and Art Director: Jeff A. Storm
Creative Consultant: Mikal Keefer
Production Manager: DeAnne Lear

Unless otherwise indicated, all Scripture quotations are taken from the LIVE *Holy Bible*, New Living Translation, copyright © 1996, 2004, 2007. Used by permission of Tyndale House Publishers, Inc., Carol Stream, Illinois 60188. All rights reserved.

ISBN 978-0-7644-3862-2

10 9 8 7 6 5   18 17 16 15 14 13 12 11 10
Printed in the United States of America.

Thanks:

Who bought this book for you?
Write a thank-you to them on this page. Tear it out and give it to the person who gave you this journal. Thank them for thinking of you and let them know you'll tell'em how it turns out.
Also let them know all the people listed on this credit page thank them, too. They contributed to us keeping our jobs.
Thanks.

Introduction

In the beginning God made perfect stuff. Including you. He provides exactly what we need when we need it so that we will enjoy life and live it through him.

But unless you've been living in the northern most point on the planet, chances are good you're living to consume and not consuming to live.

Marketing messages bombard us daily drowning out God's voice as they sell us the lies that it's all about us. The messages create a spiritual disease called materialism.

We're not becoming a disposable nation.

We're there.

And you can blame me for this assault of messages that can lead to an accumulating addiction. In part anyway.

It was because my generation of Gen Xers spent so much on stuff and cared so much about getting more stuff that corporate marketers took notice. They started spending thousands of dollars aiming the product ads right at teens.

They're still doing it—and it's working.

U.S. companies market to you with an annual budget of $15 billion. They don't blink an eye spending that much to sell you a

$15,000,000,000

lie because every year you buy it. Some analysts already estimate youth will spend $91.1 billion in the year 2011.

I remember attending Christian youth conferences and hearing speakers passionately cry out, "YOU are the generation that will change the world. YOURS is the generation that will share your faith at any cost." (And don't leave before you buy a conference T-shirt.)

I still attend youth conferences as a volunteer and often hear that same tired rallying cry drone on year after year after year.

And I see teens who remind me of me. The ones cheering the idea of changing the world as they're checking out the girl a few rows away and texting their friend about her (while wearing last year's conference T-shirt.)

Surprise! My generation didn't change the world, the generation before mine didn't, and I suspect that on a generational scale—yours won't either.

Truth —**You can't change the world without first being changed.**

Let's start changing by peeling away the layers that stand between us and passionate relationship with Jesus.

I questioned whether I was qualified to write this devotional journey, but my friend Patty inspired and convinced me that I should because—in addition to being an artist, youth volunteer, father, and friend—I'm a recovering material-holic who hasn't been sober that long.

My pulse still quickens at the word *upgrade*.

I'm not going to pose as the expert and pretend I know everything about you. Thanks to Solomon and his research journal—Ecclesiastes—we'll have a guide that walks us through what is important and how to find true joy.

Solomon's a qualified guide because he was very rich and very powerful, a have-it-all-did-that-been-there kind of guy who has great insight into doing life without God and solutions to removing selfish pursuits.

Solomon wrote that there's an opportune time to destroy and to construct (Ecclesiastes 3:3). It's time to destroy.

Each page of this 128 page journal is designed to be torn out and experienced. This devotional is an active reminder of getting past or getting rid of the layers we put between us and Jesus every day. It's time to get stripped clean.

START HERE Tear out this entire introduction. Then get a Bible—one you'll actually read. Borrow one, take one that's just sitting in the back of the church, ask a hotel desk clerk for one from a bedside dresser. If necessary, buy one.

Then fold this intro in half and use it to mark the beginning of Ecclesiastes. Find Psalms in the middle of the Bible and turn right two more books—you're there.

fold in half

It's All Smoke

Early in Solomon's life, he was faithful in honoring God and his dad, David. So one night God told Solomon in a dream, Ask for whatever you want me to give you and it's yours. Read 1 Kings 3:5 to get the full story.

That's an offer even Bill Gates couldn't make.

Solomon humbly asked for and got a discerning and wise heart. Pleased with Solomon's answer, God said there would be no one wiser or more discerning. Not before Solomon, not after him.

Ever.

And for his winning answer, God even gave Solomon what he didn't ask for. The things you and I probably would have asked for initially: riches and honor and a long life.

Later on, wise Solomon shelved God to indulge in the diversions of the world. And in the evening of his life, Solomon collected his thoughts and research in an attempt to answer this question: What is the real meaning of life?

Did you read the ending to the Harry Potter series before you read the whole book? I did.

I know, I know. But before you judge me, know that Solomon, who God made wise, did something similar by starting his journal with the ending—life under the sun is meaningless. This from the guy who had it all.

Read Ecclesiastes 1:2-11, then wrestle with these questions.

What are some things you're working really hard for?

What do you hope you'll gain from all that hard work?

Add your own page numbers if you want. ➞

If only I had (   ) I would be really happy.

Solomon's question: After all the pleasures of life are used up, what do you think will remain to satisfy your hunger for life?

Jesus asked a similar question in Matthew 16:26: "And what do you benefit if you gain the whole world but lose your own soul?"

Grab a pen

Write your ending here at the beginning.

What do you hope the evening of your life looks like?

What type of house do you plan on living in?

What kind of car will you drive?

How many Benjamins will you be pulling in?

Will you have kids? a dog? a cat? a fish? a hermit crab? a plant?

Who will your friends be?

What will you wear?

Where will you live?

What will be your job title?

What will make you happiest in 20 years?

Start burning here.

Grab some matches

After you've written your answers on this page, tear it out. As you start or end your day, read through your answers. Begin your prayer time by burning this page (in a safe place like over a sink, in a fireplace, or over an outdoor fire pit maybe). Pray that God would be your success and your happiness. Pray for a present and a future experienced with God.

FREE, FREE, FREE

There is a scene in the classic 1970's movie version of *Willy Wonka and the Chocolate Factory* where Willy, Charlie, grandpa Joe, and the rest of the guests enter what, to me, seems to be a dream-come-true-room.

Willie releases his visitors to explore the massive space informing them that everything they see is edible. Try it. Enjoy it.

How cool would it be to go into a room and eat a chocolate couch?

And yet, with all the freedom boundaries remain.

Like not swimming in the sterilized, waterfall mixed, chocolate pond—as cool as that sounds.

In the end, even sweet, innocent, humble Charlie breaks a few boundaries. Willie's account of these broken boundaries is brutal.

But it ends really well.

In Ecclesiastes 11:9-10 Solomon sounds like Willie Wonka.

Sort of.

"Young people, it's wonderful to be young! Enjoy every minute of it. Do everything you want to do, take it all in. But remember that you must give an account to God for everything you do. So refuse to worry, and keep your body healthy. But remember that youth, with a whole life before you, is meaningless."

When's the last time you had an impulse to do something and just did it?

What, if any, limits did you set on this impulse?

If you shared this impulse with Jesus, would or did the limits change?

Live free with God today.
Enjoy every minute of it.

Start by painting anything you want on this side of the page after you tear it out.

Find some chocolate syrup or coffee or whatever consumable liquid is in the house. Use that as your paint. Only limitation: paint with anything but a brush.

Let your painting be a part of your conversation with God today. Thank God for the strength and passion you have right now. Let's both ask God to guide the impulses of our hearts.

I'm free in Christ.

Winning Thought

Classic game rules: Two people take turns connecting dots to form squares. Whoever draws a line that forms a square wins that square.

This one though, is played by yourself at the end of the day.

Tear this page out and then, one line at a time, start connecting two dots with a straight line or a wavy line.

The straight line represents thoughts you had of God today or moments you took talking to Jesus. —————

The wavy line represents junky thoughts and wasted time. Thoughts of buying new stuff, how to get more money. Time spent on the Internet, in front of the TV, playing video games. ～～～～

Connect all the dots—who won today?

Read this today: **Ecclesiastes 2:1-11**.

True or false: Whoever has the most toys wins.

Advertisers want us to believe that's true and deceptively use words and images to lure us into believing more toys = happiness.

Not just more but new, too.

I've fed my quest for newness by bouncing from new thing to new thing, obsessing over acquiring more.

But the obsession isn't enough. It's never enough.

It leads to believing we'll never earn enough, never be beautiful enough, that our cars aren't fast enough, clothes not fashionable enough, gadgets not new enough, rooms never furnished enough, relationships never romantic enough, parents definitely not "cool" enough...

Enough!

Tomorrow, I choose to be inspired by God and enjoy the music on the MP3 player I already have and not be consumed with getting a newer, thinner, faster, touchy-feely, MP3 player with optional back scratcher attachment.

No matter how cool that TV ad makes the back scratcher look.

Play the line game again tomorrow. See if you can live a day where the straight lines win.

•   •   •   •

•   •   •   •

•   •   •   •

•   •   •   •

Meaningless Smarts

There is no meaning in accomplishment unless it's linked with God.

Is the key to happiness a perfect 1600 on the SAT?

I don't know if it would have made me happier, but it might have made college a little cheaper...which would have made me happier.

Or not.

Solomon aced every subject he tried, and he tried them all.

Architecture being one of them.

He was a driven and brilliant architect. The guy built several cities from the ground up, built a palace comparable to none, and built THE Jewish temple. He was renowned for his architectural abilities—which required he master math, art, physics, and language.

However, not a single one of his projects stands today.

Not one.

Without looking it up on the Internet, could you tell me who Jack Kilby is?

Clue: If it weren't for him, you couldn't look him up on the Internet.

Solomon's observation: Neither the wise nor the foolish will be remembered. Smarts won't fill the God-shaped hole in your life.

Answer: Jack Kilby is a Nobel Prize winner who pioneered the integrated circuit that led to the moon landing, personal computers, cell phones, and the Internet.

Pray for God to guide you in your pursuit of knowledge, and that he would leave his fingerprint on everything you study and learn.

Tear this page out then write a prayer in each of the subject blocks below. Cut the blocks out and place them in your school textbooks or keep them near where you do your homework.

Read a prayer you wrote every time you start to study. Pursue Jesus in every subject.

If happiness were found in education alone, then Ph.D.s would be the happiest people on earth.

Math

cut out and place in textbook

English

cut out and place in textbook

History

cut out and place in textbook

_____

(other subject)

cut out and place in textbook

Two lefts don't make a right, but three do.

What you see is not what you get

DOWN

Perception is reality, right?

Up is up and down is down. Owning the right clothes, having the right electronics, and hanging with the right friends bring happiness. Right?

Perception is part of the decision-making ability in our brains. It involves the senses, and senses are easily tricked.

I've driven past huge, 8-bedroom, 4-bath, double car garage homes with a pool out back and, staring at them, I start thinking, *man, if I had that pad, I'd be happy.* I also believe leaving my shirt untucked makes me look thinner.

Not everything you see is what you get.

You identify your place in the world partly through how you perceive the world around you. And everyone perceives the world or even a moment differently.

The beauty of this is what makes a poet passionate about words and a plumber passionate about copper pipe.

Wrong perception is believing that anything other than God can truly make us happy and give us meaning in life.

Solomon concluded that excluding God renders life meaningless.

Is your perception of yourself, God, friends, family, happiness, or meaning blurred? Why?

Tear out this page and take the visual test on the flip side. It's a classic illustration of perception you may recognize.

After you take the test, go test a friend.

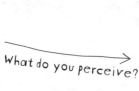

Do you see the white vase or the two faces in profile?

Eventually you'll see both. Your mind will move back and forth uncontrollably from one image to the other.

Here's the real test. Now that you have found both images in the single image, choose to stare at just one—either the vase or the two faces for at least 30 seconds, without bouncing to the other image. **Ready? GO!**

How did you do? If you're like most people, even though you chose the vase, your mind slipped into the faces and vice versa.

It is virtually impossible to keep your mind on a single perception once you're aware of an alternative interpretation.

This was a harmless optical illusion. There are alternative perception tests with real-life consequences. Like flipping back and forth between saving money and spending it or perceiving the world with God or without God.

Jesus offers "perception protection." "Then he said, 'Beware! Guard against every kind of greed. Life is not measured by how much you own.'" Luke 12:15.

(Can you imagine this verse as an ad for one of those self-storage businesses?)

Is there an alternative perception dragging your attention from Jesus?

Why does Jesus not seem to struggle with perception alternatives?

Is there real danger if we're not focused on Jesus all the time?

Nothing Better

Start or end today (depending on whether you're a morning person or a night owl) by reading **Ecclesiastes 2:21-26**.

What do you like most about Christmas?

Simple things make me happiest. Eating mom's peanut butter pie. Purchasing a gift like blankets or some chickens from the Gospel for Asia catalog for someone in Asia (last year our family bought a goat). Playing all my Christmas jazz music. Hanging Christmas lights on our house.

All of them.

They're sips of joy from God.

The really simple things, Solomon discovered, are pleasures directly from the hand of God.

He's already pointed out that our projects, wealth, and knowledge are not the ultimate meaning in life. Without reference to God, they're empty and meaningless pursuits.

Solomon decided there is nothing better than to enjoy food and drink and to find satisfaction in a hard day's work.

A bag of tortilla chips, a cold Dr Pepper, and homework—a gift?

Yes, but a caution: First enjoy God. Then enjoy his gifts.

Enjoy your stuff.

What spoils gifts from God is the hunger to squeeze more out of them than what they can give or what they were designed to give.

Work at enjoying God first every day.

Tear out this page and build a reminder to sip in joy from God.

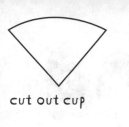
cut out cup

fold/tape

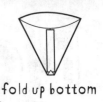
fold up bottom

cut out cup

"So whether you eat or drink, or whatever you do, do it all for the glory of God" 1 Corinthians 10:31.

Sip a cool drink from your cup and pray for Jesus to satisfy your thirsty soul. Thank God for your food, drink, and work.

$450 Billion

$450,000,000,000

$10 billion

On average, $450 billion is what Americans spend on Christmas presents, according to adventconspiracy.org.

Every year!

Adventconspiracy.org also estimates that it would take $10 billion to provide clean water.

For everyone!

Today's prayer is simple, but the challenge is not as simple.

Thank God today for the clean water you have. Pray for those people who are suffering disease and death due to the lack of clean water. Selfishness is a layer that can be removed when we act on behalf of others.

Read ECCLESIASTES 2:11.

Tear out this page.

Spend some time with these questions then take the
$10 billion challenge.

Jesus said that when he is with his Father, anyone who believes in him will do the same things he did and even greater things. (John 14:12)
  Can you list an example of someone doing greater things than Jesus did?

  Solomon says we can't see the whole scope of God's work from beginning to end. Does that make it easier or harder for you when you're trying to do what God wants you to do? Why?

  In the world of business, success is measured by profit and goals completed. As Christians, how do we measure success in the things we do for others?

The Challenge: For two weeks drink only water, and then after the two weeks, send the money you would have spent on soda or coffee to an organization that is building wells in the poorest parts of the world that suffer from impure water or drought.

Tear out this page and put it in the refrigerator—let it be a reminder not only to drink just water for two weeks, but also that God can multiply every gift we provide.

REMINDER
Just H2O for 2 weeks

THINK TWICE

Debt is a disease that can be very hard to cure. Families and individuals can suffer from it. Entire countries struggle every year to get out of it. Ironically, even credit card companies are suffering from it.

For some the cure can begin with a very simple practice to curb the habit. **THINK TWICE**.

My dad, who has gone through bankruptcy due to credit card debt, to this day struggles with not falling back into debt.

The disease is tough to cure if you suffer from spending addiction and are not in the habit of thinking twice before buying stuff.

You know you're on your way to contracting the disease if symptoms that seem harmless are not treated early.

Symptoms like:

The belief that having new things makes you happier.

Believing that you deserve to live beyond your financial means.

Feeling the need to have as many or more new things than your friends.

You don't save any money, or you don't save for necessities.

You obsess on getting the latest upgrade.

Your first thought is to replace and not to fix.

You feel you never have enough money.

You lose sleep thinking about how to buy or get something new.

Read Ecclesiastes 5:8-20.

If there is one person to believe about wealth, it would be the wealthiest person in the world. No, not Warren Buffet. The wealthiest person who has ever or will ever live—Solomon.

Enjoy what you have. Spend more of your life pursing what God has given you and not what God has not given you. Joy can be swallowed up by the pursuit of more and new. Think twice.

Tear out this page.

Tear out this page and the next 2 pages. Tear out the THINK TWICE labels and start putting them in places where you'll come across them, or where people in your family will come across them. In your wallet, in your purse, next to the TV, in a pair of older shoes, in the closet, on your desk, in your clothes drawer...

Let them serve as reminders to start curing or to avoid the spending addiction. As you place labels, pray for God to guide you in how you spend money. Thank God for the gifts he has given you, and ask him to keep you busy enjoying life.

Cut out these labels.

THINK TWICE

THINK TWICE

THINK TWICE

THINK TWICE

THINK TWICE

THINK TWICE

THINK TWICE

THINK TWICE

THINK TWICE

THINK TWICE

Try This

Quitting bad habits cold-turkey rarely works.

Smokers use the nicotine patch to wean themselves off cigarettes.

Chunky guys, like me, try curbing our midnight appetites by drinking more water and eating fewer donuts for dessert.

Nervous habits like chewing your nails might require removing some stress from your life before you can stop eating your own fingers.

Getting over the urge to buy and consume is just as hard to quit. It requires steps.

Tear out this page and turn it over.

Take some baby steps

30-Day Wish List

Write down the things you really want to buy. New jeans, MP3 player, bobble-head of your favorite Bible character...whatever.

Tape this list to a calendar or give this list to someone you trust like your mom. Ask that person to give it back to you in 30 days.

If you are still wanting these things, ask yourself why. Evaluate your savings and research the best possible deal if you do decide to buy.

If you have lost some of your enthusiasm for buying something on the list—let it go.

Try this same method for cleaning out stuff you already have.

Take and closet some of the things in your room or in your life that are just collecting dust. If after 30 days you forget about them and never use them—let them go.

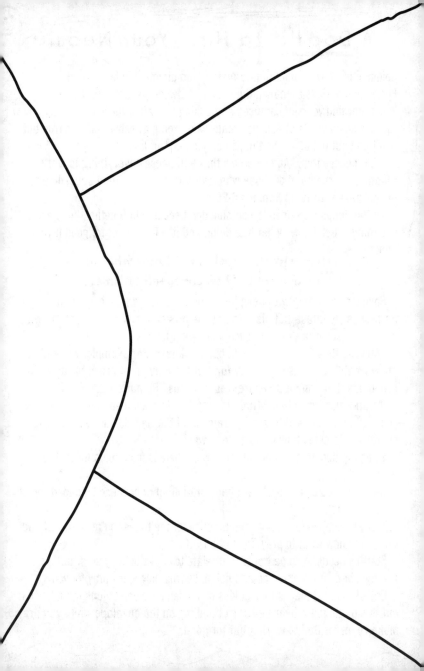

A Doodle to Help Your Noodle

Solomon is weaving a lot of information and direction in his journal Ecclesiastes. He is even including some "between the line" imploring. You might find yourself confused and asking how all of these things work, how these wisdom words of Solomon really work. You may sense they are true but don't understand all of the things going on in your life.

First, believe this, **"And we know that God causes everything to work together for the good of those who love God and are called according to his purpose for them" Romans 8:28.**

All the things we see on the outside don't seem to fit together, but we know one thing—God knows what he's doing and it will work out for good if we love him.

Then why do we still not know what to do? Why are we still so confused at times?

Solomon is sharing with us in his journal that God's plan is good, his purpose is steadfast, but his methods are mysterious. Knowledge starts with prayer. But sometimes I don't even know what to pray.

"And the Holy Spirit helps us in our weakness. For example, we don't know what God wants us to pray for. But the Holy Spirit prays for us with groanings that cannot be expressed in words" Romans 8:26.

As an artist, when I am struggling for a really good idea and nothing is coming to mind, I need to get my brain out of the way. So I doodle. I let the creative right side of my brain go for a walk.

When I'm doodling, I'm out of the way so there is more room for God to work in me.

BAM! An idea comes out that I had not thought of because I stopped trying to take control.

Today's devotion is a suggested practice for the times you're confused and you don't know what to pray. Try it often.

Start by doodling some words that relate to or symbolize your situation, feelings, or confusion. Let go and listen. Let the Holy Spirit pray for you.

One of the best places to doodle is on a used envelope or junk mail. **So tear out this page, flip it over and start doodling on the envelope while you pray. Make room for God to work it out for good.**

PARENT CONTRACT

Mom and/or Dad, I am trying to spend less on meaningless items that I know won't bring me true happiness. And do you know where much of that money comes from that I am now trying to spend less of?

You.

Some of the $600 billion my peers and I spend every year on clothes, electronics, music, software etc., comes from my allowance—from you.

I'm trying to be stripped clean of things that get between me and Jesus, and in that effort I could use some help.

I am asking you to sign this contract that will keep us both accountable this next year and, if signed, means we both take this seriously.

1. You will spend less money on stuff for me and spend more time with me.

2. That _____% of my allowance will be donated to a cause of my choosing.

3. We spend more time this Christmas making things together and less time shopping for random, meaningless gifts. (Making things can include but is not limited to presents, dinner, time, memories.)

4. You include me in some of the family buying decisions.

5. I will help pay for _____ with money I save or earn.

6. We will discuss a reasonable budget to be kept by both you and me.

7. You will spend roughly 60 days reading through Ecclesiastes as I am doing.

8. You will pray with me no less than 3 times a week this year.

Any reluctance to signing this contract will be discussed openly by all necessary parties. Please sign below.

_____

On This Day_____Month_____Year_____

This contract is a legal Stripped Clean document.

Please tear out this contract and have it signed by all concerned. Then display this contract somewhere all parties will see it and not lose track of it. If this contract is not displayed as a constant reminder, it is neither binding nor will it do much good as a reminder.

An 'ok' Story

I bought my daughter a popular MP3 player for her birthday but didn't pay very close attention to the minimum requirements for using it.

First mistake.

When I tried to launch it from our computer at home, I discovered that my operating system was too outdated to use the new music player.

I went to the computer store to see about getting an operating system upgrade only to discover it would render my current software unusable. I'd need to upgrade all my software, too. But the new software wasn't built to work on my dated computer. Grrrrrrrrr!

So after careful evaluation, and seeing how dated all my computer stuff has become, I decided to invest in a new computer.

After pricing the system and all the software upgrades, I determined that our family budget would allow for only the computer and not all the software upgrades.

Then, the week before I purchased the computer, I got news of a hardware upgrade coming the following month. So I waited.

Four months later I don't have a new computer and my daughter still hasn't used her new music player.

If that's not enough, the MP3 player I bought has already been upgraded to a thinner, colorful, music, movie, game player with even more memory.

I curse the concept of upgrade.

I've lain awake at night thinking about how I could sell the player I bought and invest in the newer one. I'm trying to erase the feelings haunting me that I'm a terrible dad whose gifts to his daughter are lousy promises that don't work.

When I sat down with my daughter to talk about selling the player, upgrading it in a couple of months after we maybe have a new computer, here's what she said.

"Dad, I don't want a new one. I just want the one you bought for my birthday. It's OK, we'll get it working eventually. It's OK, dad."

Yes, my eyes started leaking.

My daughter gets it.

Tear out this page and turn it over.

Why do we spend so much time and energy pursuing NEW?

Jesus said not to be too concerned about perishable things (John 6:27).

What does "too concerned" look like for you?

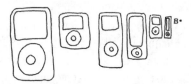

 TRY THIS

Tear out this page then cut out the shape to the left. Roll it up to make a straw. Try using it today to take a drink.

Drinking from this straw is hard. You can get the liquid refreshment, but there is a desire to quit, or you'll want to get a new plastic straw or just gulp it down without a straw at all.

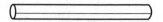

It's hard to keep from wanting "new" all the time and trying to satisfy our selfish wants. We're bombarded with messages that new is always better and makes us better.

Pray today for God to make you a new creation in Jesus, and to help you with the struggle of not being too concerned with perishable things.

Cut on dashed line

Roll ⟶

What do we want? Freedom. When do we want it? Now.

If words alone were enough, then why are stop signs red octagons?

A stop sign is designed to capture your attention and communicate clearly. Its size, color, shape, and wording work in harmony to get you to do something that just might save your life.

When a group of protesters gets together to protest, they don't just use bullhorns and annoying chants. They also use signs to get peoples' attention. Protest signs.

Their signs use color, shape, and a few words to communicate how they really feel. It lets the world see how passionate they are.

I almost got in a car accident once while trying to read all the protest signs from members of a local union, who were on strike and picketing next to a busy intersection.

I could grasp their opinion and passion from reading the few words on their signs.

If there were a protest against the Pharisees, would Jesus—who called the Pharisees snakes, whitewashed tombs, and hypocrites—make a sign that had these words on it and join the protesters? Matthew 23:1-33

Tear out this page and turn it over.

Use this page to build a protest sign. As you peel away layers that crowd between you and Jesus, what sin or bad habit are you going to start protesting in your life? As you re-energize your passion for Jesus or develop a passion for him for the first time, what are you going to do to fuel that passion?

Build a protest sign with a few words that represent your need for Christ and what it is you are stripping clean to get closer to him.

Feel free to walk the streets hoisting your sign high. We are free in Christ.

Or post it on your bedroom wall for everyone who enters your domain to see.

Let it help communicate your passion for Jesus.

Design. Cut out. Post.

For Guys Only

Girls—tear out the next two pages and give them to your older brother or a guy friend.

Early on in Solomon's journal we discover everything is meaningless without God. Wisdom, wealth...no matter how much more we acquire, we always want more. Never content.

Guys, that couldn't be more true when it comes to pornography.

Sexual sin is a highly addictive layer between us and Jesus.

As an adult I have yet to meet a guy who has found true happiness in pornography or sexual sin, or a guy who's never struggled with sexual sin.

Solomon tried to find meaning in sex and beautiful concubines. He lived a "rock star" life for a time. **Read Ecclesiastes 2:8**. Solomon denied himself no pleasure. See 1 Kings 11:1-3—Solomon's affairs with many foreign women never satisfied the need for a deep relationship or provided any real joy.

One of God's most beautiful creations is woman. As a student in art school, I learned early on why many of the great masters drew and painted the female figure. Their form is one of the most beautiful in nature.

Porn turns that beauty into an ugly illusion. An illusion that becomes addicting and can destroy the true joy God intended for sex.

God's love can overcome the sin. Just check out the story of David.

Read 2 Samuel 11:2. David noticed a woman of unusual beauty taking a bath...David's sexual desire led to having Bathsheba's husband killed so he could have her for his own. After being confronted, David received forgiveness, but not without consequence. God's love overcomes the struggle.

Conquering porn addiction is a lifelong fight with temptation, but God is faithful and he'll provide strength, endurance, and support.

God intended sex between a married couple to be a beautiful experience. It's a gift of pleasure, devotion, and intimacy between a married man and woman.

Anything outside of that is not how God intended sex to be experienced. It's an easy gift to corrupt if left to our own selfish desires.

Continually watching porn corrupts your relationships right now, and it also damages your relationship with your future wife—even before you're married.

Porn creates dangerous expectations for you and your spouse. Wives feel like they can never satisfy their husbands and that they're never beautiful enough. Guys start comparing themselves to what Craig Gross, pastor of xxxchurch.com, calls "sexual athletes." Trying to be something God never intended them to be.

At its worst, guys start substituting watching porn for actual sexual relations with their spouses. Trust shatters and relationships suffer.

You simply won't be able to get enough. Satisfying sexual urges on your own becomes a dangerous substitution.

Solomon learned that pursuing selfish sexual desires not only breaks God's heart, it also tears things apart that are hard to put back together.

The list of forbidden sexual practices in Leviticus 18:1-30 is a graphic warning to guys. Add to the list watching Internet porn and downloading porn to your cell phone, and it's still just a list of don'ts you can read on your own.

One of the most popular excuses from guys, even Christian guys, is that they've tried to stop looking on their own, but they're always pulled to watch—just one more time. It's a struggle not easily conquered by yourself.

Confide in your youth pastor, a parent, a grandparent, someone you trust. Someone who'll walk with you and keep you accountable. No matter how hard you try, or how hard you pray, the pull to look just one more time is more often than not stronger than we are.

Check out xxxchurch.com to download Internet blockers, read testimonies, get prayer, and find other resources to help you move past the addiction.

Tear out this page and then tear it up into pieces. As you start your prayer time, try taping the pieces back together.

Porn tears up our relationships with others and with God. And it's really hard to try and put the pieces back together ourselves. We need Jesus to give us a second chance. We need Jesus to mend our brokenness.

Tear out this page and fold it up as small as you can get it.

Then put the folded piece of paper in your shoe. Put your shoe on and go through your day. That uncomfortable feeling is a reminder to pray. Ask God for help as you struggle to get away from sexual sin and to stop the desire for porn.

List on the other side of this page some people you can talk to about this issue—and then talk to them. Commit to it. Don't let it go. (1 John 1:8-10)

It's uncomfortable to have this page in your shoe, and it's uncomfortable to confess sin. Don't believe for a second that sexual sin goes away as you get older. Do the hard thing. Now. Every guy struggles with this. Not every guy comes clean. Remember: Nothing can keep us from the love of God.

Read it.
Know it.
Live it!

"So now there is no condemnation for those who belong to Christ Jesus. And because you belong to him, the power of the life-giving Spirit has freed you from the power of sin that leads to death."

Romans 8:1-2

I am going to talk to this person and ask them to walk with me in this battle against sexual sin.

_____

_____

Pray for God to bring you out of any sexual sin you might be in now or to protect you from getting into it. Pray for the strength in pursuing purity. Pray for your future spouse that she would be free from sexual sin. Pray for strength and that God would put the right person in your life to help you fight the porn addiction.

You can do this.
You are not alone.

For Girls Only

Guys—tear out the next two pages and give them to your older sister or a girl friend.

It has to be hard being a girl and, at the same time, being satisfied with the way God made you.

Advertisers spend billions of dollars trying to convince you that your clothes are never new enough or that they fit you just right. That expensive make-up will make you more beautiful. That buying brand-name accessories will get you noticed. Advertisers and peers alike often have you questioning whether you're thin enough. Your natural cycles are the butt of television jokes, boys may lure the "love" carrot in front of you so that they can have sex with you and criticize your worth if you refuse.

The message: Girls are supposed to be perfect—and you fall short. Physically. Socially. In every possible way.

Solomon (not a girl) has two insights for you (a girl).

Read Ecclesiastes 3:11-12 today.

You are beautiful to God right now. With your braces. With zits appearing without warning. Without the latest and greatest fashion accessories.

You're beautiful to God right now, just as you are. You're loved no less or no more than you'll ever be loved by God.

Which leads to Solomon's second insight for you:

Read Ecclesiastes 6:9.

Going through life striving for rewards or the applause of others or accumulating more stuff will not make you feel better about yourself—for long. That road eventually leads to disappointment—guaranteed.

Comparing yourself to the computer manipulated pictures, the straight A student, the girl with all the boyfriends will bring frustration and regret.

So why waste your energy on the attempt and pin your hopes there?

Maybe it's a better idea to seek contentment?

True success is faithfully pleasing God with the resources and responsibilities he's placed in your life right now. To enjoy what and who you are. Right now, as is.

Culture tells you it's essential that you be perfect. Perfect looks. Perfect poise. Perfect talent. Perfectly perfect.

Except you aren't. And striving for perfection—with the payoff of gaining the attention and approval of others—is meaningless.

"Don't be concerned about the outward beauty of fancy hairstyles, expensive jewelry, or beautiful clothes. You should clothe yourselves instead with the beauty of a gentle and quiet spirit, which is so precious to God" (1 Peter 3:3-4).

Tear out this page and then tear it into 3 pieces. Wad up the 3 pieces and attempt to juggle them to start your prayer time today.

The wads of paper represent desire for physical beauty, self-esteem, and success.

You may actually be able to juggle all of them for a moment, but the emphasis on juggling them at all is meaningless.

Pray for a gentle and quiet spirit. Pray for God to shower you with his recognition, and ask God to help you stop chasing the wind by looking at everything but him for fulfillment.

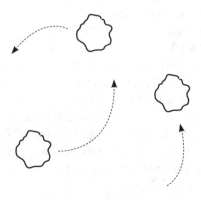

Statistically girls take longer showers than guys and take considerably longer to get ready for the day.

I live with girls so I know this. I'm also bald, so maybe that explains some of the time difference, too.

Even if this is not the case for you, shower time is still a great time to spend with God. A time to focus on what you like about yourself. And to ask God about how to enhance and share those qualities.

Tear out this page and write a few things that you really like about yourself. Are you a good listener, committed to staying sexually pure, good with kids, athletic, a good student, artistic, musically inclined, have a fun sense of humor, appreciate a really good meal?

Write down those attributes on this page and take this page into the shower with you. Wet it. Stick it to the shower door or shower wall.

While you're in the shower look at the list and praise God for the gifts he's given you. And thank God for seeing you as a beautiful daughter.

Be inspired. Feel good about yourself. Be content.

Wash away thoughts of doubt and low self-worth. Be invigorated by the Holy Spirit pouring out his love for you.

Qualities and gifts

Stick this side to the

shower door or wall.

Happy Death Day

There is a layer between us and Jesus called the I'll do it tomorrow layer. I'll start worrying about my reputation when I'm an adult—after I've had some fun. I'll enjoy life—after I get enough money. I'll follow Jesus—later.

Any of these cross your mind lately?

Read Ecclesiastes 7:1. Sounds pretty depressing. But know that Solomon wrote 8 times in Ecclesiastes that we should enjoy the life we have.

Here's some valuable info to help understand this verse.

In Hebrew the word for *name* is *shem* and the word for *perfume* is *shemen*. Solomon is making a play on words. Possibly to get our attention.

Kinda' like if I were a popular mushroom, I'd be a fungi. Or maybe not.

Anyway, Solomon is saying there are two days in your life when your name is prominent—the day you receive your name, and the day your name shows up in the obituary.

What happens between those two days determines whether your name is a sweet smelling ointment *shemen*, or stinky and forgettable.

If you die with a good name, you can no longer do anything to screw that up. But the day you get your name, the day you are born, you have an entire life ahead of you that is yet unwritten.

Looking back on a life well-lived is better than looking forward to a life unlived.

Therein lies the layer. Your *shem* started when you were born and doesn't take a vacation while you're a teen. The type of odor your life emits includes what you do with it right now.

What good are you doing with your youthful powers now?

If you just met Jesus and were going to lunch with him, what is one thing you would want him to know about you right now?

Write your name really big on this side of the page.
Then write down one thing you can do starting today that
will be a fine perfume to God.

- -

Spray some cologne or perfume on this page. Then
fold and tuck this page behind your student ID or drivers
license. Let it be a reminder that your life can be sweet
smelling to Jesus by how you live it. Right now. Let that
be your prayer today.

PAIN
Is Such a Rush

Read Ecclesiastes 7:3 today.
Solomon says we are to live and enjoy life, also to take life seriously and don't let it slip through our fingers.

Solomon, wise Solomon, learned something in his pursuit of life without God. It's a tough truth but here it is: It's easier to learn from adversity than from prosperity.

Wisdom grows as it's refined in the fire of sadness and pain: having sex before marriage, parents divorcing, the pressure to succeed, the death of a friend or family member...I could go on for pages.

You may have grown angry with God, and that's OK. He knows all about pain. And like marathon winners know, strength comes from pain.

Pain is not a sign of weakness. It's an exercise of your faith muscle. And when life hits bumps, faith muscles get a workout.

Our highest purpose is not to be happy. Our purpose is to live life with God. To know and enjoy God. And knowing God sometimes involves pain.

Nick Vujicic is someone I respect. A lot. He is a living, breathing testament to Ecclesiastes 7:3.

Nick was born without arms or legs, and his story includes sharing his love of Jesus with the entire world. He shares how pain and suffering shaped his life, his heart, and how it has solidified his faith in God. Check out his story at lifewithoutlimbs.org.

If strength comes from pain, why did Jesus spend so much time healing people of sickness and physical conditions?

When was a time pain increased your faith?

What would you tell someone experiencing a pain you suffer or have suffered?

Tear out this page and post it somewhere you can read it daily, like on the bathroom mirror. Or share it with someone that you know is in pain.

Brief History: Horatio Spafford composed this hymn.

He wrote it shortly after a ship carrying his wife and daughters sank in the Atlantic ocean. All four of his daughters drowned.

He composed the hymn while passing through the area his daughters drowned just days before, as he headed to be with his grieving wife.

Let the words be your prayer and your hope.

When peace, like a river, attendeth my way,
When sorrows like sea billows roll;
Whatever my lot, thou has taught me to say,
It is well, it is well with my soul.

It is well with my soul,
It is well,
It is well, it is well, with my soul.

Though Satan should buffet, though trials should come,
Let this blest assurance control,
That Christ has regarded my helpless estate,
And hath shed his own blood for my soul.

My sin, oh, the bliss of this glorious thought!
My sin, not in part but the whole,
Is nailed to the cross, and I bear it no more,
Praise the Lord, praise the Lord, O my soul!

And Lord, haste the day when my faith shall be sight,
The clouds be rolled back as a scroll;
The trump shall resound, and the Lord shall descend,
Even so, it is well with my soul.

"It Is Well With My Soul" by Horatio G. Spafford.

Pain Part 2: Suffering

Enjoying life and having fun is, well, fun. But we learn more from adversity than we do from prosperity Solomon tells us.

The deeper learning moments in life often happen in times of disease, destruction, and difficulty.

I rarely talk to God about the deeper meaning of life and what it's all about when things are going really well. I suspect that if you're honest, I'm not alone.

It's when we're told by a family member (who provides the only income for the family) that he or she has been diagnosed with cancer and life expectancy is just a few months, that we start asking the hard questions of God. It's times like that when our faith is really stretched.

When wise people face adversity like this, they take to heart the lessons learned and become better instead of bitter.

It's a choice that's made in the heart, and those who choose to live by faith are driven to God in desperation.

A person who says he or she never hit bumps or appears to be living a smooth, easy life with an uninterrupted pattern of success is missing the stretching of faith and trust muscles.

Nothing but fun doesn't teach much of anything about the nature of life. Solomon notes that thinking otherwise leads us into pretending that happiness can make us whole.

Pain truly changes us, and great men and women are shaped by pain.

Is someone in your life being changed by pain? How is that person changing?

Jesus healed people by just touching them—why didn't he heal himself when he was beaten and crucified?

Unless you spend a lot of time pretending to be happy, you'll suffer pain. And it can leave you bitter or better.

Pain and suffering that separates you and Jesus can be stripped away by the decision to be better for it.

Tear out this page and scratch on the blackness something that represents a painful time or suffering moment. Maybe it's the name of someone you love whose suffering is really stretching your faith or maybe even building up bitterness between you and God. Maybe it's a date.

After you scratch the name or incident, take a deep breath and pray a simple prayer.

God, I know there are no guarantees in life except for one. You promise to never leave me alone. Whatever I am going through, you will go through it with me.

Jesus, you understand pain. Being beaten, abandoned by all your friends, and nailed to a cross. And you overcame it.

You know my pain. Please bring peace and take away the bitterness. Let me know you are there. Let me fall into your arms. Amen.

Buddies

Super heroes call them sidekicks. Lawyers call them partners. Employers call them employees. They're called spouses, brothers in the hood, teammates, buddies...they're all collaborations.

One of the best collaborations is friendships.

And not the illusion of friendship some think exists between them and the 200+ list of people on their Facebook page.

There's a layer between us and Jesus called the I'll do it myself layer. It shows up various times in our lives, but always leads back to the same place: No, you can't.

There was a popular response to rhetorical statements in the latter half of the 20th century: Duh! A one-word way of saying "no kidding" or "that's so obvious."

I think *duh* originated in Ecclesiastes, Solomon's journal.

Read Ecclesiastes 4:7-12. The term *duh*, was born in verse 11.

It seems so obvious, yet we do everything we can to accomplish things on our own. Maybe it's out of conceit. Maybe it's because we're raised thinking that real success is all about becoming a winner on our own. Or maybe it's because someone told us we couldn't do it. Whatever the reason, Solomon's right: We can't do it on our own. And one of the challenges in forming good friendships is that they take time.

It takes time to establish a friendship with someone who'll stay by your side, even when it's your fault, or someone you can text when you're hurting, or one who always seems to have your best interests at heart. Or even a friend who would lay down his or her life for you (John 15:13).

Tear out this page and turn it over.

How are your friendships with others like a friendship with Jesus?

Is there something preventing you from starting at home and having a sibling or parent as a good friend? How can you collaborate with a family member to improve your friendship?

Whether you're trying to develop a new friendship with someone or you need to encourage an existing friendship—reaching out to others with something as simple as a thank-you can help grow the relationship.

Tear out this page

Wrap a gift of thanks with it. Then give it to a friend or potential friend. Thank that person for being there for you...or hanging out with you at the concert...or listening to you...whatever.

Guys, you can even do this without it being "girly." Maybe you wrap up a piece of jerky and offer it to a friend to say "thanks" for not being a jerk to you.

GUY IDEA #2: Buy tickets to the Friday night girl's volleyball game and wrap them in this page. Include a note saying you'll bring the Dr Pepper if your friend brings the air horn.

GIRL IDEA #1: Girls are better at giving thank-you gifts. I think you have it covered.

Thanks...

A Real Layer of
Inauthenticity

Read Ecclesiastes 7:17-18 today.
Some have interpreted these verses to mean that living a moderate Christian life is good.

Don't be very good, and don't be very bad.

Let's hear it for mediocrity. Yaaa! Whoooo! I don't think so.

Have you ever given the "relationship by association" answer when your actions are questioned? You know, when you're asked about your Christian life you answer, "I'm not as bad as some and I'm not as good as some. I guess I'm OK."

So what says Solomon?

It's not about being partly good and not totally bad. It's about being authentic.

Don't go around bragging how wonderful you are and don't be falsely humble either. Don't be a show-off Christian acting spiritually conceited.

Righteousness put on public display turns into self-righteousness.

But there's more.

Don't get comfortable with sin because of a past failure. If you've had sex, been drunk, taken illegal drugs, been a thief...don't embrace a lifestyle of sin and impurity because of that moral failure in your past.

Sin can become the stick we use to beat ourselves into believing we can't be forgiven and loved by God because we screwed up and "hey, my friends are doing worse stuff than me, so I'm basically OK." Comparing our sin to other's sin doesn't excuse ours.

The things you say, the things you do, the decisions you make should represent what is in your heart. Authentically.

In Christ there is no condemnation. **Reads Romans 8.**

Tear out this page

If you're a Christian, know this: Going to church every Sunday, doing a Bible study, hanging with the youth group, talking Christianese...none of these makes you authentic.

Your attitude toward others, your grace toward others, your love for others... that's the evidence of authenticity.

Solomon even gives the formula for becoming authentic. **Read Ecclesiastes 7:18.**

You and I need to fear God.

Not like scary, hide from him, always think he's out to get you fear. Rather, it's a high regard kind of fear. High regard for the one who knows all and sees all and who really recognizes how our hearts can be motivated to be self-serving.

Sincere reverence for God drives us to authenticity.

Jesus, who is our model for authenticity, touched people with contagious diseases, and spent time in rough places with rough crowds. Being authentic and loving people sometimes ended with his life being threatened.

If you are struggling to be authentic, what is it that you fear more than God?

Tear out this page and use it to serve someone today.

Use it like a rag and clean up someone's spill.

or

Wash someone's windshield with this page.

HIGH RISK: Use this page to clean up someone's bathroom.

or

Serve someone a snack on this page.

Use this page to serve someone. Let your prayer time be filled with thanking God for providing you what you need to serve and asking for even more ideas and opportunities to serve and be authentic.

SUPER POWER

Wisdom won't solve everything, but it does have power in it. It doesn't answer every question—but it does give you perspective.

Perspective on life's struggles and on being authentic.

Read Ecclesiastes 7:19-22 today.

Fear (awesome reverence) of God leads to power. So much power that you don't have to fear other people at all.

If the center of our fear sphere is God, we can honestly face our struggles with sin. Our answers come from God.

Wisdom strengthens and makes you and I even more powerful.

Peeling away the layer of worrying about what other people or circumstances are saying happens when God is truly the center— each and every day.

It's your super power and, like Superman who uses the sun to recharge, we need to recharge every day.

I have been so upset by what others have said about me that I retaliate with the same hurtful words instead of love. I mirror what was done right back at them. I forget the golden rule and don't do unto others what I want done to me. I'm left standing in the reality that I often hold others to a higher standard than I hold myself. You may resonate with this.

Tear out this page and turn it over.

Today you'll take a challenge to test your super power.

First though, pray and get charged up.

WARNING: Do not try this without praying first. You may like what you hear and you may not like what you hear and, in both instances, may find what others are saying about you to be kryptonite.

So pray. Pray for wisdom and for strength today. Today your worth and confidence comes from the wisdom of knowing Jesus.

Here is your power verse for support.

Read Ephesians 4:21-24. "Since you have heard about Jesus and have learned the truth that comes from him, throw off your old sinful nature and your former way of life, which is corrupted by lust and deception. Instead, let the Spirit renew your thoughts and attitudes. Put on your new nature, created to be like God—truly righteous and holy."

Test your super power—Fold this top part backward then tape this page to the back of your shirt . Put on the shirt and go through the whole day wearing this sign, and let people write on your sign.

Fold top part over.

WHAT DO YOU THINK OF ME?

WRITE IT HERE.

Enjoy Life Today!

Ecclesiastes 5:19-20

Pray a prayer of thanksgiving today. Thank God for the breath of life you enjoy today. The layer to strip clean today is the layer of worrying about yesterday. A past sin, something you screwed up, a bad day a day ago.

Today starts with a decision. Either it's "good Lord, morning" or "good morning, Lord." It's a clean start today. Pursue God with confidence.

To help you get started, **tear out this page,** turn it over, then cut out and fold the feel-good twirler. The only additional part you'll need is a paper clip.

After you get your twirler built, pray as you throw it, thanking God for the day and for letting you enjoy it. Thank God for another chance to pursue him and let him fill the needs of your day no matter how it turns out.

Tear out this page.

1 Peter 1:8

Bottom Flap

A

B

Cut solid lines, fold dotted lines. Fold in A then fold B over A. Then fold up bottom flap. Place paper clip over A & B to keep bottom flap folded.

Fold C away from you. Fold D toward you.

C

D

Hold bottom paper-clipped section and throw like a paper airplane. Let the twirling fun begin.

Draw on your twirler something God has provided you that brings you joy.

DEATH
The Great Leveler

Let's deal with death, Solomon style. Not ignore or fear death but face it—as a friend and not our enemy.

Our response to death tells a lot about us. **Read Ecclesiastes 9:4-6**.

Solomon's not suggesting there's no hope for life beyond the grave, instead it's where there is life and hope!

It's better to be a live dog, a despised animal in Judaism, than a dead lion, the king of the jungle.

You can deal with death by ignoring it as if it ain't gonna happen. Reality says otherwise. It's the only 100% guarantee in life.

Or you can look at life as the precious thing that it is, and while you are still alive have hope. Hope of meeting God face-to-face someday, the hope of living significantly right now, the hope of doing something to the glory of God right now.

Solomon points out things we can't do once we're dead. But we can do them while we are alive. We can love or not love. Instead of ignoring death, be reminded: While you live and breathe you can live a life connected to God. We can love like God. Right now.

So take stock of your time, and do something with it now because there's a time coming when you won't be able to do anything Solomon suggested.

There's no "do overs" after you're dead.

I don't think Solomon is suggesting we face death so we'll be scared or discouraged and depressed.

He's asking you and I to look death in the face, step back and evaluate what it means for us right now.

Take a look at your life through the lens of death. What will be left behind? Solomon's description of a person who has died is a view of death without God. He says they know nothing, they have no reward, they are forgotten, and nothing they have done has any significance. They have no more share in anything that's done under the sun.

So what good are you doing now, connected to God, that can be passed on?

Tear out this page and then look death in the face by writing out a will. List what you will leave behind. What will you pass along to others?

I,_____being of sound mind leave behind:
  (name)

Will you leave behind a 2-year-old computer or a legacy?

A lawyer will review a will to make sure it's accurate. If Jesus reviewed the will you just made, would he find it accurate? If not, what do you need to change, right now?

LIFE
The Party Before Death

You looked death in the face—now what?

Read Ecclesiastes 9:7-10

OK, if you read those verses, I think I know what you're thinking. You're possibly thinking an all night drinking party with tons of pizza has been God-approved.

Am I right? That's what I was thinking at first.

Solomon is not saying since you are going to die, go out be merry, eat, and drink yourself into a stupor so you won't have to deal with it.

He is telling us to stop moping around and get up and enjoy the life God has given us.

So eat every meal like you are at a banquet! OK, you're going to die someday, but you're going to eat lunch today. Eat it like it's a banquet.

And it's not the food you eat, it's the attitude you bring to the table.

Family dinner table, burger corral, picnic table...it doesn't matter. Just get to the place where every meal is a banquet. Sit, listen, and enjoy who's at the table with you.

Once you're able to see the shortness of life, let it motivate you to take advantage of the life God has given you.

What about the party part? Well, in the culture of Solomon, special occasions—parties—were important to the entire family. Everyone would put on their dress whites and splash perfume all over their bodies.

Solomon is saying we should always be clothed in white and always be anointed in oil. Don't just celebrate on special occasions. Celebrate every day!

You are alive. You have a lot to celebrate, so make every day a festival.

But wait. Dressing in white is always a symbol of purity, and the oil is commonly a symbol of the Spirit of God. So party well—enjoy life with all your energy in the purity and power of God.

Tear out this page and the next 2 pages and use them to help make your next meal a banquet. With family, friends, small-group...remember it doesn't matter what the food is—simple or complex, it's the attitude you bring to the table.

Share with your guests why you are having this "banquet." You might even plan a meal and treat it as a banquet with friends or family.

Enjoy every good thing from God including your earthly gifts, and ask for his guidance to rightfully use them.

Some things to help get your any-time-meal, CELEBRATE LIFE banquet started.

Discussion starter coaster. Cut out and put on table.

Why do you think the first miracle Jesus did was turning water into wine?

Does that seem worthy of his power and mission?

tear up the page after you cut out the coasters and use as party confetti

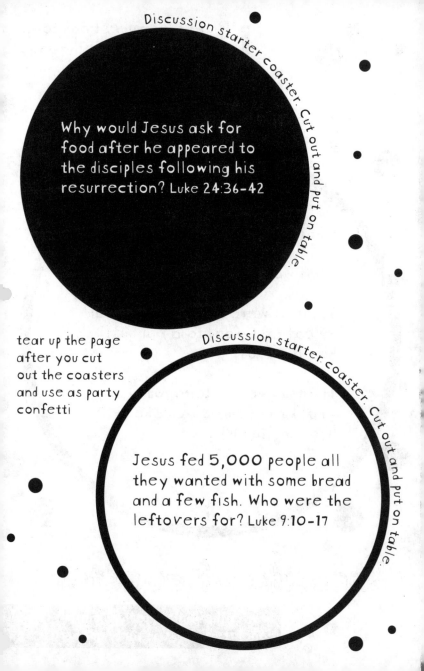

Discussion starter coaster. Cut out and put on table.

Why would Jesus ask for food after he appeared to the disciples following his resurrection? Luke 24:36-42

tear up the page after you cut out the coasters and use as party confetti

Discussion starter coaster. Cut out and put on table.

Jesus fed 5,000 people all they wanted with some bread and a few fish. Who were the leftovers for? Luke 9:10-17

! Write these questions down before you tear up the page for confetti.

More banquet discussion starters.

What's your favorite food? Why?

What would be your ideal party?

If Jesus were born in 1985, would he eat fast-food today or just healthy food?

If Jesus were a teen today, what kind of music would he be listening to? Why?

Backside of coasters

tear up the page after you cut out the coasters and use as party confetti

Jesus miraculously provided food when he was around crowds. Why didn't he provide food this way at every meal?

cut out and photocopy as many as you need or email the invite or send as a text message or call...

You Are Invited
to
A Banquet Celebrating Life

Be My Guest

When:

Where:

! Write these questions down before you tear up the page for confetti.

More banquet discussion starters.

Jesus ate meals with a lot of different people. Do you think the conversation was him teaching the whole time?

Do you think Jesus cared about his hair cut, length of his beard, or what he was wearing?

If Jesus were to use a movie to tell a story (parable), would it ever be an R-rated movie?

Backside of invitation

tear up the page after you cut out the coasters and invitation, then use as party confetti

WORK
Ecclesiastes 9:10

Remember the statistic of $600 billion of spending by youth? Much of that money comes from teens who work after school and during the summer. And most of those teens are working to acquire electronics, clothes and/or a car.

Maybe you're one of them.

Here is a stat that my pastor shared with me. By the time a person is age 50 if he or she has worked full time since college, they will have put in 56,000 hours of work.

What if all that time could be devoted to God or God's work?

Ya, if you were a pastor or missionary. **Read Ecclesiastes 9:10**.

But no. Solomon says whatever you do, do well...Colossians 3:23 says it this way—"Work willingly at whatever you do, as though you were working for the Lord rather than for people."

And because life is short and unpredictable, Solomon urges us to approach work with passion and excitement.

Life is a gift and Solomon tells us that work is, too. So how can we work for God in whatever we do and earn money for stuff?

One suggestion is attitude. Service and ministry are not the only things tied directly to God. If it's honoring to God, you should do it full hearted.

Sweep the floors, clean the bathrooms, talk with the customer...Just get up every day and say, "This is yours, Lord. In all I do I want to honor you."

The most profound example of this is my dad. A hero of mine.

For 40+ years he worked in a steel mill making pipe. Sure, he bought us kids toys for Christmas, owned a couple of new cars over the years, and we took a few vacations. But what my dad talks about now after retiring is the pride he has in the steel he made and about the guys at work he shared Jesus with or guys he prayed with or for. Work was an opportunity he was given by God. An opportunity he used to honor God.

Go to work like it's your last day to work. If you're a student, go to class today like it's the last time. If you work after school, do it to honor God.

Whatever you do, devote it to God.

Here is a quick reminder today.

Tear out this page and glue whatever you have in your pockets to the page. As you pray today, let this be a reminder that God will use whatever you do and that life is wide open for each opportunity we are given, no matter how big or how small.

Glue stuff here!

Life is designed to teach you and me humility...if we are willing students. Its lessons are constant and will beat the crud out of us if we don't cooperate.

In Chapter 8 of Ecclesiastes, Solomon shares the things that make us humble and, with the proper attitude (there's that word *attitude* again), we can start removing the layers of self-dependency that keep us from trusting God.

Read Ecclesiastes 8:1-7.

The first step to this knowledge of humbleness is the realization of our own ignorance and our trust in God's goodness.

I had an organ removed recently from my body, and if you've ever had surgery, you know what I mean when I say "you are not in control."

From the nurse who starts your IV to the doctor who puts you to sleep to the surgeon opening you up, I know what I don't know and I submit to the knowledge of the surgeon. I trust I will wake up after the procedure.

It's kind of the same in life. I'm trying not to be worried about the things I can't comprehend because I am trying to trust in the wisdom of God.

So what is true humility, really?

The pastor at my church, pastor Gary, says it this way.

"Humility is coming to grips with the fact that what we know is such a small, infinitesimal part of all that can be known, so that if anyone thinks they are educated and that makes them a candidate for pride, they just need to reassess."

Solomon says that when we have true wisdom, it comes from God. We don't have a stern face worried about what we don't know. We have a shining face because of the God we do know...and love!

Tear out this page and use the helper questions to create a poem about being humble that will, as Solomon suggests, give you a shining face. A confidence in God—not worries in what you don't know or can't explain.

Fill in the blanks to the questions or statements on the left, then write a poem using the words you added.

Keep the poem with you for a few days.

My Humble Poem

When I think of <u>God</u>
I see the image
of_____ →

I don't understand
_____ →

I trust
_____ →

I move <u>through
life</u> as if I were
_____ →

My friends would say
I'm _____ ↗

When I look at <u>myself</u> I
feel_____ ↗

<u>Jesus</u> is providing me
with _____ ↘

God
- - - - - - - - - - - - - - - -
- - - - - - - - - - - - - - - -
- - - - - - - - - - - - - - - -
through life
- - - - - - - - - - - - - - - -
- - - - - - - - - - - - - - - -
myself
- - - - - - - - - - - - - - - -
Jesus
- - - - - - - - - - - - - - - -

Live With It

I can't stand cooked spinach, I hate when people suffer under horrible dictators, I'm not real crazy about Mondays, and I wonder why the president doesn't ask me directly what I think.

Read Ecclesiastes 8:2-15.

We are caught in a world controlled by others and not ourselves. Or so it seems.

Maybe you, too, have faced the day realizing you'll have to do some stuff you don't want to do, live in a way you don't really want to live, and experience things you don't want to experience.

When I'm in a situation where I feel I have no control, humbleness sets in.

Solomon's word picture comes down to this—keep the king's command because of your allegiance to God, not because you like the king. Even when you don't understand what the king is doing, and you're not even sure you agree with it, humble yourself before authority for the sake of your allegiance to almighty God.

Not to the point of violating God's standard, though.

The book of Acts tells us that it is better to obey God than to obey man. But if you're like me, most of our problems with teachers or government are not like that. Most problems with authority are things like...cooked spinach should be banned along with weekend homework, and the speed limit should be higher.

Humility is acceptance. Accept that there are things you can't change.

Like death. You can't beat physical death. But the wealthier some people get, the more control they think they have.

I read again recently of a rich guy who is having his head cryogenically frozen in hopes of attaching it to a new body in the future. Just accept death.

Or how about the guy sitting next to you in class who gets high praise and recognition, but you know he's a cheat and jerk. He gets public praise when everyone knows that he is not what he pretends to be.

Accept it and don't get bent out of shape about it.

Or what about the girl who shakes her fist at God. She says she lives her life this way and nothing's happened yet. And nothing's going to happen.

Except God is not on our time clock. His debts have not come due yet. There will be a day of reckoning, so don't be fooled by the success of evil people.

Life is filled with distress, and Solomon says it is the wise person who understands and accepts that.

Learn how to change the stresses you can in your life, but live with and accept those stresses you can't change. Don't let them rule your life or steal your joy.

The further you are from God, the less you talk with him, the less you lay down before Jesus, the more distressed you'll become. Maybe you've already noticed this.

Tear it out

Tear out this and the next 2 pages. Wrestle with the questions on this page and the next 2 pages then wad them up into balls. Use the third page as a target that symbolizes your relationship with Jesus.

Throw the wadded up balls at the target. Step back and do it again. Step farther back and do it again.

How far away can you be and still hit the center of the target?

How is the target like how you treat your relationship with Jesus?

How is this experience like your prayer life?

Wad this page up!

What is causing you the most stress in your life right now?

Can you accept it or change it? How?

"Don't worry about anything; instead, pray about everything. Tell God what you need, and thank him for all he has done. Then you will experience God's peace, which exceeds anything we can understand. His peace will guard your hearts and minds as you live in Christ Jesus." Philippians 4:6-7

If we believe this verse to be true, then why do we still worry about stuff?

Wad this page up!

When Jesus, distressed in the garden, asked his Father if there was any way for him to avoid the cross, what do you think was going through his mind?

We learn obedience through suffering, and Hebrews says Jesus learned obedience through things he suffered. Why did Jesus have to learn obedience? (Hebrews 5:7-9)

Wad this page up!

Totally going south

Losing control

I think I have a handle on things

With Jesus
Don't worry

Hang this target on your door or wall.

Back side of target.

"You must have the same attitude that Christ Jesus had. Though he was God, he did not think of equality with God as something to cling to. Instead, he gave up his divine privileges; he took the humble position of a slave and was born as a human being. When he appeared in human form, he humbled himself in obedience to God and died a criminal's death on the cross."
Philippians 2:5-8

Mysterioso

Read Ecclesiastes 8:16-17.

God did not accidentally forget to tell us some things. God has concealed some things from us. He knows the secret stuff, and only in him can we be the discoverers. Only in him can we find the true meaning in life.

And Solomon knows that even after we ask for wisdom and seek wisdom and get wisdom, there are still going to be things that we just won't know.

Why is this? What's the point?

Mysterious stuff in life for me includes why would just a couple of degrees change in the earth's rotation cause such catastrophic results? Why does chocolate taste so good? How is it that about every 5 days I have clean socks and underwear in my drawer? And folded?

The thing is that with all my unanswerables and imponderables, I'm driven to God.

If we could understand all about life and God, then we would not be aware of our own deep shortcomings. We would not be humble and recognize the awesomeness of God.

Solomon is trying to tell us no matter how much we think we know, don't get cocky. Not even the wisest people discover everything, no matter what they claim.

I'm not going to wrack my brain about why chocolate tastes the way it does. I'm just going to enjoy the gift.

I know my wife provides me with clean and folded socks and underwear, but it's the deep love she has for me that I don't always fully comprehend...why she does it week after week. I do ponder about ways I can love her back the same way.

Solomon's observation about wisdom and humility is really deep, but it's a huge relief when he recommends we shouldn't get down about the things we don't understand. Instead, we should have fun because "there is nothing better for people in this world than to eat, drink, and enjoy life."

Enjoy this life God gave you. My thoughts are not God's thoughts. There are some things that are just too deep to understand. But God knows, and that's what makes me sit back and relax. I don't need to know everything in order to have fun and enjoy life. My comfort is trusting the one who does know it all.

There is more, beyond this life, that can be discovered in Jesus.

It's Jesus who said:

"Don't let your hearts be troubled. Trust in God, and trust also in me. There is more than enough room in my Father's home. If this were not so, would I have told you that I am going to prepare a place for you? When everything is ready, I will come and get you, so that you will always be with me where I am."
John 14:1-3

Tear out this page

How many dots would it take to fill the box below? Using a pen or pencil, start filling the box with dots. Try it. Was your guess even close?

It's a simple reminder that only God knows the secret things, and only in him can we be the discoverers.

After you try filling the box with dots, spend some time in prayer today and bring the things that are confusing you, are a mystery to you, or that you want to understand but don't, to God. Thank the Creator for all the good gifts he gives you and for giving you wisdom in his perfect timing.

SERVICE DAY

Today put some humility into action. Spend the day serving others. Do something for someone else today. Buy them lunch, wash their car...If they are not quite sure why you are serving them, share this page with them.

You'll be able to share it with them because you'll be wearing it.

Tear out this page and find a way to wear it throughout your day of service to others.

Be creative.

Form it into a tie.

Let it hang out of your back pocket.

Make it into a bracelet.

"You must have the same attitude that Christ Jesus had.

Though he was God, he did not think of equality with God as something to cling to.

Instead, he gave up his divine privileges; he took the humble position of a slave and was born as a human being.

When he appeared in human form, he humbled himself in obedience to God and died a criminal's death on the cross."

Philippians 2:5-8

My Plan, God's Steps

Read Ecclesiastes 9:11-12.

Maybe you've already noticed this: The best person doesn't always win. At least not at first.

I watched a short video on the history of Pixar animation studio. Part of the story is about John Lasseter, who directed *Toy Story*, *Cars*, and other films.

John Lasseter was a huge fan of Disney at a young age, and he wanted nothing more than to be an animator for Walt Disney Studios. He even got a job, when he was a teen, sweeping the streets in Tomorrowland at the Disney theme park in California. He moved up to being one of the ride operators and started meeting all the "right" people in the Disney organization.

He went on to study animation after high school and won several awards for his student work. One of his first real animation jobs was at, you guessed it, Disney Animation Studios. He spent a lot of sleepless nights trying to move up the ladder at the studio and eventually landed the privilege of directing his first full-length animation.

After presenting what he felt were really good story boards and noting that digitally animating the picture would not cost any more than the traditional 2-D animation, he was fired. Disney executives were not ready for digital animation.

Solomon tells us even if you think you've done everything perfect in this life and have all the necessary skills, brilliance, and integrity, you will not be automatically rewarded.

Sometimes the things that happen to us are not about our abilities or our skills or our readiness for the task, but it's about timing or the opportunities given us. The steps we take in our lives are mostly unknown and could change our whole pattern of existence at any time.

God reminds us over and over that we don't know the future, but we do know who holds the future and that the best person doesn't always win.

So hold on to God with all your might no matter what comes.

I don't know if John Lasseter knows this truth, but he did continue to pursue his dream and eventually created and directed the first full-length digitally animated film, *Toy Story*.

Not all of us will see our successes broadcast around the world, but Solomon isn't telling us to give our best and work with all our might toward a goal for public success.

He told us there's real joy in our work and the success of our work. Whatever work it might be. Solomon's insight is that the results from all of our efforts and plans are not in our control.

"We can make our plans, but the Lord determines our steps" Proverbs 16:9.

Keep working towards a dream. Keep trying to excel at school and at sports and whatever else God has set before you, and be reminded by Solomon that success in the rat race is not ours to command.

Tear out this page.

Write out your prayer today and then put it in your Bible.

Write down a dream or goal you have. One that you want to accomplish now or one you're working toward in the future.

Now add these words to the end of your goal...*if this plan fits your plan, God. If not, please let me know what it is I should do and how to get there.*

....

....

....

Remembered

Tear out this page.

List below everything you think is on a penny.
Now find a penny and do a rubbing of it with this page and a pencil.

....

....

Do the rubbing here.

Read Ecclesiastes 9:13-16.
How did you do? What didn't you remember was on a penny?

There is yet another layer that gets thicker and harder to beat the older you get if you don't figure out a way to deal with it when you're young. It's the layer of craving to be noticed. Often.

You make good choices, you don't get caught in the trap of accumulation and materialism, you give your best every time, and now you want a little recognition.

Solomon would share with this person how impressive that is—but a good person is not always noticed or remembered.

The parable that Solomon shares in Chapter 9 tells a lot about what people are really like.

If we go through life seeking recognition and applause, we'll not only be disappointed, but we can become addicted to the effort. It's a waste of energy.

I often get caught in the addiction for approval and thinking the good I do will actually get noticed and bring me some glory.

I try to impress others with my little successes, my new purchases, and even with how much my service is noticed.

Think I'm bad? Check out Hollywood celebrities or those Christians who feed their addiction by making a spectacle of their service efforts. They make sure everyone sees them doing the right thing.

Paul points out that recognition is not what makes us strong.

"That's why I take pleasure in my weaknesses, and in the insults, hardships, persecutions, and troubles that I suffer for Christ. For when I am weak, then I am strong" 2 Corinthians 12:10.

Solomon's message to me is to spend more energy recognizing God in my life and less time trying to get noticed. No matter how good I am.

Victor David Brenner was the only sculptor invited to render America's first portrait coin in 1909. Brenner was a respected and gifted artist and singled out by President Theodore Roosevelt as the most talented artist to do the rendering of Lincoln's face on the penny. The only remaining recognition of this great artist on the most recognized American coin are 3 microscopic initials at the bottom of Lincoln's shoulder.

Application for a Balanced Life

We are all seduced in the rat race of life—striving to get ahead or get the next thing.

Too many times we miss out on the joy of a balanced life. Why does it seem so difficult to remember what Solomon keeps telling us? Enjoy this life and know this isn't all there is.

The picture Solomon keeps painting in Ecclesiastes is that he searched out every possible way to find the meaning of life without God (under the sun) only to find himself grasping for the wind. It's meaningless.

The alternative word picture Solomon paints is to lean on God's strength (over the sun). Know that he is in control and use whatever abilities God has given you. Live by God's instructions and his view of life.

Then whatever comes our way, whatever challenge or trouble, we know who remains in control. We know who we can trust. We know who is not shaken.

You can remain faithful to God because he is faithful.

A good definition for faith is believing God tells the truth.

Tear out this page. Then take the application test on the other side for "an above the sun" perspective on the rat race.

This is not a test you should take once and forget about. Put this page somewhere you can review it often.

Cut out the test and put it somewhere you will see it every day. The one place that comes to mind is the toilet. Find a way to get this into a bathroom you use routinely, and daily spend some time reviewing this test.

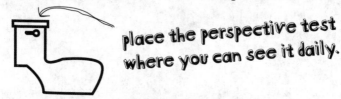

place the perspective test where you can see it daily.

1. Do I regularly spend quality time alone with God?

2. Do I have goals for—
My personal life?
My involvement in church?
My involvement in community?
My education?

3. Am I willing to put aside pursuing a more "luxurious" lifestyle for better relationships with my family and friends?

4. Do I check my plans and resources often to see if they are in line with God's will?

Intermission

Solomon looks back over his life in the book of Ecclesiastes, which is, as I mentioned earlier, a sort of journal of his existence and his evaluation of life under the sun—telling us what life is like when God is not in the picture.

If you have at least read and evaluated some of the devotions in this book, you, too, are able to take a look at your life right now and really start asking yourself some tough questions about meaning in your life. What is it that you are holding on to for contentment? pleasure? accomplishments? wealth? Or are you finding meaning with God as your guide?

Solomon spends the first 9 chapters of his journal deconstructing and demolishing the things "under the sun" that we tend to hold on to, thinking they give life meaning. Solomon is also the searcher, trying to find meaning in living life without God.

Conclusion: Life is uncertain. In their right place, there are things that bring us joy in life. But without God we only end up with regrets, meaninglessness, and "grasping at the wind."

Solomon is going to turn a corner on this journey. Now that we have had an opportunity to start removing some of the layers between us and Jesus and discovering ways to keep those layers from crowding back into our lives— Solomon is going to use that cleared space and help us start planting and rebuilding.

So before Solomon starts laying down another proverb to help us understand the difference between being wise and being foolish, let's take an intermission.

Tear out this page and flip it over.

Do whatever you want to with this page except throw it away.

Read Ecclesiastes 10:1.
The first step in rebuilding is understanding the difference between being wise and being foolish.

The picture Solomon paints in this verse ties in to a previous picture he painted early on in Ecclesiastes about our lives being a sweet perfume.

A fly is pretty small, but if it dies in the perfume box—that won't be a Ralph Lauren or Calvin Klein fragrance you're smelling.

In a similar way—a little bit of foolishness in our lives can destroy the perfume of our lives. It can destroy a reputation.

Solomon's picture demonstrates that it doesn't take a big mistake. We can be foolish in little things.

You don't have to do anything huge to mess up your life, just do some little thing and watch the results.

Throughout the Bible are warnings about these little things that cause massive damage.

"...Don't you realize that this sin is like a little yeast that spreads through the whole batch of dough?" 1 Corinthians 5:6.

"In the same way, the tongue is a small thing that makes grand speeches. But a tiny spark can set a great forest on fire" James 3:5.

Solomon says that you don't want to take the little things for granted. Be careful that you don't assume that one little thing doesn't matter.

The wrong conversation with a guy who is not your boyfriend, the wrong website, the wrong hurtful word, the little bit of gossip. A little thing can bring on great damage.

Be sensible about the little things.

Tear out this page and fold it as small as you possibly can.

As you fold, remember the little foolish things that can make for big problems.

If it would be a helpful reminder to you, put the folded up sheet into your pocket. When you take it out and unfold it, let it be a reminder how the little things can be big disasters.

Pray today for God to give you the wisdom and opportunity to not do one little thing that can undercut all that he is doing in your life right now.

EXTRA: Before you fold this page up **Read Ecclesiastes 10:2-3**. What is it about the right side?

In Solomon's culture, a person's right hand was perceived as the place of power and a person's left hand as the place of weakness. It's not to pick on lefties, it's just another word picture. The illustration is that one little sin can be a big mess for all to see.

Don't worry, lefties; righties are at risk of the same consequence for a little sin.

Just wanted to make sure that was cleared up before moving on.

The Difficult Things

Read Ecclesiastes 10:4-7 today.

Solomon saw it; maybe you've seen it, too. The ego-driven leader who promotes unqualified people and ignores the good people all around him.

Maybe there is someone in your circle of friends or teachers or job supervisors who thinks they are above everyone else and walks all over you, your talents, and isn't fair at all. What about that student leader or adult who keeps ignoring you even though you work really hard—you're never recognized.

That makes me angry. How about you?

Solomon gives us some counsel to deal with these difficult situations that keeps us sensible and wise in those difficult times.

Don't panic, don't quit your job, don't leave your position. Deal with it according to Scripture, and don't act out of anger. Be patient and deal with it in a sensible way, a godly way first.

"Patience can persuade a prince, and soft speech can break bones" Proverbs 25:15.

"A gentle answer deflects anger, but harsh words make tempers flare" Proverbs 15:1.

Maybe you've done this? After getting walked on verbally by someone, you get in the car, and while going home you start giving yourself a speech on how you'd like to take that guy and...

Or did you model Jesus? When people throw their insults at you, you just entrust them to God.

It doesn't seem fair when wicked people prosper. It doesn't seem fair that godliness isn't always rewarded or integrity is sometimes ignored.

It can make us bitter toward God. Even to the point of finding ourselves acting in the same way toward others.

We see this stuff, live with this stuff, and recognize that sometimes that's just the way life is.

It's those times I have to remember who loves me in spite of my shortcomings and anger, then talk to God about it instead of someone else.

Solomon's counsel...

"Never make light of the king, even in your thoughts. And don't make fun of the powerful, even in your own bedroom. For a little bird might deliver your message and tell them what you said"

Ecclesiates 10:20.

Be sensible, be disciplined when it comes to the difficult people and difficult situations in our lives. That's Solomon's reminder to us.

Jesus used a whip when he drove the money changers out of the temple. Does Jesus endorse violence as way to deal with people who anger you?

Tear out this page. Write down a difficulty you are struggling with right now or write down the name of a difficult person you are dealing with. Instead of growing angry about the situation or person and unloading on someone else—stop and give it over to God. Pray and ask him to change the situation or the person and to give you the patience to deal with it. When you're done praying, flush this page down the toilet or throw it away.

Leave it with God, then let it go. Fall back into the arms of Jesus by having a good conversation with him today.

Here is a visual reminder that illustrates our need to be patient in difficult situations and to rely on God who is unshakable to work it out.

Make this a devotional time with God as you entrust him with the difficult times and people in your life.

Tear out this page and turn it over.

Tear out page. Cut solid lines. Then unfold without breaking apart the ring.

Starting with your head, pull the paper loop over yourself.

Keep going until your entire body has passed through the loop without tearing it.

When it comes to difficult people and difficult situations, be sensible and wise.

"We also pray that you will be strengthened with all his glorious power so you will have all the endurance

and patience you need. May you be filled with joy, always thanking the Father" Colossians 1:11-12.

Sharpen Your Ax and Wear a Hard Hat

Read Ecclesiastes 10:8-11.

It's believed that this section of Scripture can be interpreted that Solomon is pointing out the things that can happen in the workplace when workers are foolish.

That could easily mean school, too.

Bottom line—when you go to work or to school, put your head on. If you don't you could find trouble really quickly, and Solomon gives 5 illustrations of this.

Sometimes asking for guidance before you're in trouble will eliminate potential joy busting layers between you and Jesus.

With the examples of being bitten by a snake, a stone falling on a guy's head, and a guy using a dull ax, Solomon is indicating to us that we should wake up every morning and ask God for wisdom to handle the day.

Wisdom to handle the challenges we have at work and at school because there are dangers and risks.

Solomon has already pointed out that we are to enjoy our work and life and do them both well.

If the wood cutter in Solomon's word picture would have taken some time to sharpen the ax, he would not have had to work so hard.

Don't seek advice and help after you're already in the ditch is another way of looking at this.

Get some correction and guidance from someone you love before it's too late.

Tear out this page and turn it over.

Sit down with a parent or both parents sometime this week. Ask them some tough questions. Use this time to get their opinion on something difficult you are dealing with or anticipate dealing with in your life.

Ask them what was one of the most difficult times in their life and how it turned out.

Ask about a sin they struggled with as a teen and what was the result.

Ask them what was the hardest thing about being a teen. How did they deal with it?

Write down their answers and tuck this page in your Bible.

Tear out this page. Then write on this page
some hurtful words you have used this past
week. Write down some foolish comments
you've made to someone. Write down some
hurtful thoughts you had about someone.

As you pray today asking for wisdom and help
avoiding foolish or hurtful comments, start
poking holes in the page. Remember that even
the smallest mistakes destroy joy in us and in
others.

"In the same way, the tongue is a small thing that makes grand speeches. But a tiny spark can set a great forest on fire" James 3:5.

How to Lasso the Tongue

Read Ecclesiastes 10:12-15 today.

He puts his foot in his mouth so often, he has athletes tongue.

Every time she opens her mouth, she spews stupidity.

Why can't he keep his big mouth shut?

There are probably even more ways of putting it. You see it in movies, read about it in stories, see it played out in people around you, and sometimes it's even you. The fool with the hit-and-run tongue.

Solomon knew it, Jesus knew it, James knew it...the tongue is harder to control than that bag of bottle rockets I accidentally lit all at once.

Deep wounds can be inflicted with the words we use. Sometimes I can hear it in my heart—God telling me to keep my big mouth shut—but I can't count the times I've ignored the voice.

Solomon has already said there is a time to speak and a time to be silent, and now Solomon is trying to make it really clear that we don't have any idea how much damage our mouth causes sometimes.

Trying to be funny I actually asked my sister, who was suffering some weight gain due to some stressful life situations, when she was due to have her baby.

I know now.

God really wants us to have a good and enjoyable life. That's the message Solomon has delivered over and over again. Life is so much more enjoyable if we actually try to be sensible.

Getting wisdom involves working together with God in a cooperative effort.

As you pray today, think of times when the words you have used caused others pain and made you the fool. Pray for wisdom to have better control of your tongue.

Pray for God's help—that his spirit would continue speaking to your heart when your brain keeps trying to convince you to say something when you should be silent.

To help you focus while you're praying, (tear out this page) and place your tongue in the circle. Keep this page on your tongue while you pray out loud.

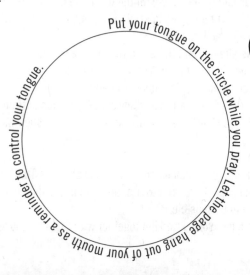

Put your tongue on the circle while you pray. Let the page hang out of your mouth as a reminder to control your tongue.

Tongue Control
Part Deux

Read Proverbs 2:1-5.

How many times have you been in a situation where you are biting your tongue while walking away because you said the wrong thing the wrong way to the wrong person at the wrong time?

There are a lot of layers between us and Jesus in the form of selfish words or hurtful words. Sometimes we'll say just about anything if we think it will help us win the argument.

Ever been embarrassed publicly by someone, and in your head the moment turns into a video game where your thumb starts to hurt because you're pushing the fire button furiously firing off word bombs at the person who hurt you? Or does that just happen in my head?

Anyway, Solomon points out the damage our tongues can cause, and James adds how hard it is to control our words of pain.

"We can make a large horse go wherever we want by means of a small bit in its mouth. And a small rudder makes a huge ship turn wherever the pilot chooses to go, even though the winds are strong. In the same way, the tongue is a small thing that makes grand speeches" James 3:3-5.

Tear out this page and flip it to the other side.

Keeping the layers of hurtful words from crowding out Jesus in life requires guarding your tongue and being sensible. It also requires working at it all the time.

The tongue is a small thing but it can cause a lot of damage. It takes work to guard your tongue. It's not easy.

Write out a short prayer asking for strength and wisdom to control your tongue. Write your prayer with the pen in your mouth. Like guarding your tongue, it's not easy.

"Indeed, we all make many mistakes. For if we could control our tongues, we would be perfect and could also control ourselves in every other way" James 3:2.

Read Ecclesiastes 10:15.

Weight lifters that are building muscle to lift more weight and not interested in sculpting their muscles will often do what I've heard them call a blowout.

They lift as much weight as they can, as quickly as they can, for as long as they can. They do this to the point of complete exhaustion and tear up so much muscle tissue that they can't bend their arms to tie their own shoes.

The thinking is that as the muscle tissue heals after a blowout, it grows and becomes more dense thus making it possible for weight lifters to increase the amount of weight they can lift.

I've watched this event take place a few times in the gym. As I watch these guys do blowouts, a couple of things go through my mind.

Thought 1: Man what idiots these guys are. Tearing up their bodies so they can lift more weight, so they can do more blowouts. Seems pointless.

Thought 2: Wow, that's cool. They will give everything their bodies can dish out for something they are passionate about.

Solomon, in one verse, tells how a fool (one who refuses God's teaching) grows tired laboring for temporary things and endless pursuits.

That focus and energy spent on no real purpose exhausts the fool.

Getting rid of the layers between us and our relationship with Jesus requires more than the occasional, whispered, 30-second prayer you don't quite finish because you're drifting off to sleep.

Let's do a blowout with purpose and get our prayer life stronger so we'll desire to pray even more, ask God harder questions, and take every single issue to him laying it at his feet.

Tear out this page.

A respectable leader would not ask others to do anything he himself was not willing to do.

That goes for this exercise. I'm not asking you to try something that I have not tried or am not willing to try again.

I have grown weary because of wimpy prayers and have to ask myself when was the last time I got exhausted praying.

As a teen, I got exhausted talking with my girlfriend on the phone. I now experience times when I get exhausted from beautiful, long conversations with my wife (same girl I talked with as a teen, by the way.)

It's love that drives you to those great exhausting times. It's passion.

That same passion for Jesus drives us into great exhausting conversations. But sometimes if your prayer muscles get a little limp, a good blowout gets them back in order.

Design a "Do Not Disturb" sign with this page. Hang it on the door to your room or bathroom. Close the door and start praying to the point of exhaustion. Lay it all at the Cross. Listen and fall in love again with Jesus.

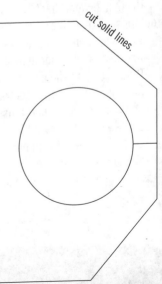

cut solid lines.

Be Bold

Solomon has investigated life and tried all of life's possibilities without God, and the results are all the same. Never being fulfilled. Never being content. Never being truly happy.

But in the latter half of his journal, Ecclesiastes, Solomon takes all that he learns and gives it away to us in the form of principles on how we can find joy.

Solomon is going to point us in a better direction and a way to live life "under the sun." A way that can keep us from having a life that is empty and meaningless.

While we're on this earth, there are layers of junk between us and Jesus that need to be removed and priorities set up so we can continue removing the layers when we allow them to re-enter our lives.

Read Ecclesiastes 11:1 today.

Solomon paints another word picture that may have connections to foreign commerce of his culture.

Ships were put out to sea in search of gain from the venture. Someday they would return after an unplanned period of time with something to show for the risk.

In comparison, guys and girls who trust God must venture out in life, courageously. Even when the picture of the future is not complete, but there is a knowledge that there is a dependable order and plan to the venture, that God will work everything out for your good.

God's control of our lives is our strength.

In Solomon's word picture, *to throw* suggests the idea of throwing ourselves toward something. Which has an element of adventure. You don't necessarily know what is around the corner or what the obstacles will be. But we can trust God to help us face the battles and storms we will encounter.

Conclusion: If there are risks in life, and there are, then isn't it better to fail in venturing forth than to remain on shore in safety?

Tear out this page.

Write down the things that you fear most. Things happening right now or things you fear will happen.

Fear is a layer that Jesus knows we have, and he really wants us to hold on to him and not the fear. Venture forth because Jesus really does have your best interests in mind.

Paul reminded Timothy, his protégé, of this.

"For God has not given us a spirit of fear and timidity, but of power, love, and self-discipline" 2 Timothy 1:7.

Peter knew that if we launch boldly into life, there is power if we launch with God and trust in him.

"Give all your worries and cares to God, for he cares about you" 1 Peter 5:7.

Take this page with your fears listed on it and form it into a paper airplane.

Then from the highest point you can get to, launch your plane into the wind. Launch your fears into the wind as you pray giving them up to God and asking him to help and guide you into living a bold life, even when you don't know what's going to happen next.

I fear...

Bold and Totally Committed

Read Ecclesiastes 11:1 again today.
For such a short verse, it really is packed with a lot of meaning. Something a really wise person like Solomon has no trouble doing.

The NLT Bible translation of this verse uses the word *grain*, but other translations say *bread*. A word picture for our livelihood, the sustenance of life.

Venturing forth is only half the picture. The call from Solomon is to cast off or venture forward, investing your very life in what God has put before you.

Investing your time, energy, and, yes, money into what matters. Eternally.

There is something implied in this metaphor. Solomon is challenging you and me to invest ourselves (our bread), our whole lives, our very sustenance, in what really counts for something.

So we cast ourselves to God in trust. Cast all your resources while leaving behind the fear. Sometimes I'm left wondering if my investment will come back home. Since I don't know, I wait.

You may spend a lot of resources in a relationship, in study, in constantly trying to improve your character and not see the profit from that right away.

Solomon has been suggesting throughout his journal to wait. Wait on the one who is in charge of it all. Reward always requires patience.

So we wait. Hang out in the waiting room and continue casting yourself with all your vulnerabilities upon God. Even when God never seems to be early, we can rely on him to be right on time.

Wait time unknown.

Tear out this page.

On this page and the next page write down where you are going to spend your resources this year. What are you going to cast yourself toward with all your vulnerabilities and weakness? Improving a relationship? Committing to serving someone less fortunate than you? Improving the bonds with your parents? Following God's direction for college and career? What?

Then go and hang the pages on something outside. A tree, a cactus, or a potted plant. Let it remain as a reminder to wait and pray expectantly.

Pray right now for God's guidance in your life and what it is you are supposed to cast your ship toward. Pray for patience.

As we wait for the seasons to change and bring back the leaves or the fruit, or the bloom, or the green of the grass, we wait on God. Know that he is faithful. Even though we don't know exactly when the first fruit of spring will arrive, we trust that God will bring fruit.

Write it down. Cut it out. Hang it outside.

- -

Just Wait.

Venture of Faith ⃝

....

....

....

....

Boldly Living ⃝

....

....

....

....

Jesus was "amazed" at two things: How much faith or how little faith a person displayed. Why would Jesus be amazed by this? (Luke 7:1-10)

If Jesus walked the earth today, and you sent him a text message begging him to come visit you and heal you from a terrible disease, how long would you wait before giving up on the idea he was coming? (John 11)

Bring It On, Life!

Read Ecclesiastes 11:2-3.

Solomon, in the pages of Ecclesiastes, has told us about the uncertainty of life and repeats it several times...We cannot know.

There is a classic crossroad in this life if you know for certain you are going to heaven.

You know life is uncertain and choose the road to doing nothing. Sit back and wait and let life happen to you. Do what you have to do to get by and wait for heaven to come.

Or you could choose the other road. You understand that life is uncertain and your response is, "Bring it on."

Solomon suggests we take the "bring it on" road. Give your love away, completely. Give away grace, completely. Give forgiveness, completely.

Because life is uncertain, Solomon suggests we don't fear what might come and hide. Confront it and pursue it. Invest in life even when the possibility remains that things may go the complete opposite of where you think.

Solomon reminds us again, because it is so very important, to not let fear paralyze us. Be bold and live life with confidence...not confidence in what you think you control, but confidence in the God who is in control.

Can you change the weather, taxes, test questions, final ball game scores, people's responses, time, death? Sure, we can worry about them, and I'll confess, I worry about these and a whole lot more. But I'm reminded that no matter how much I worry about the what-if's, it won't change a thing.

Solomon comes to our side and says, hey, don't worry about where the clouds dump water or which direction a tree falls, you can't control it.

But the truth in faith is that God is in charge and he asks us to trust him. Trust that the tree fell exactly where God needed it to fall.

Bethany Hamilton, a young amateur surfer, lost her arm to a 15-foot tiger shark off the coast of Kilauea, Hawaii. Instead of hiding, Bethany stepped up to life and said she's "glad this happened to her because now I can tell the whole world about God."

(http://www.christianitytoday.com/tc/2004/002/7.09.html to read more about Bethany)

Wrestle with these questions for a while.

What is it in your life that represents safety and security apart from God himself?

{ Hint: It is whatever you put your trust in, especially when life gets a little rough. It's whatever makes you so comfortable you don't want to give it up, even if it means getting closer to God. }

What area of your life are you hiding from fully and courageously trusting God?

{ Hint: Fear will probably tell you what it is, and leaving it behind may be the hardest thing you ever do. }

Growth is sometimes paid in fear. Growing may mean stepping into something totally new, taking new challenges in places you can't control. Growing almost always involves a choice between risk and comfort.

For me, this is a really hard chapter to live by. It's a struggle to remove this layer every day. Maybe it is for you, too. If I'm more vocal about my need for God, it does put a different spin on my response to God. Try this...

Tear out this page. Then roll it into a cone, a megaphone of sorts. Pray today for strength and courage and for opportunities to put those into practice. After you pray, use your megaphone to yell out to God, be bold and not afraid, to yell out how much it is you need and love Jesus.

Be extra bold and try this in public. Try something new with God. Let's both try leaving fear behind every day.

Do you see imperfect conditions or do you see life? If we insist on certainty or favorable conditions before living life, we'll never do anything. Listen to Solomon's hint of urgency.

Read Ecclesiastes 11:4.

Like the farmer who can't wait for ideal conditions before planting, Solomon is insisting that we can't wait either for perfect conditions before we serve.

We can't wait for perfect conditions to repair a relationship or wait for everything to be safe before serving God. If we wait to plant, we'll never reap a harvest.

You and I can't know what lies around the corner, but we can trust that God is in control of all. The rain, the sun, the tornado, and the famine.

This sense of urgency to live life now and not wait is seen throughout the Bible.

"Make the most of every opportunity in these evil days" Ephesians 5:16.

"Remember this—a farmer who plants only a few seeds will get a small crop. But the one who plants generously will get a generous crop" 2 Corinthians 9:6.

Now is the time to invest your life and resources into someone. Who or what is God guiding you to pour your life into? Start now because the pattern for living life boldly and removing layers of fear is often set for the rest of your life when you're young.

Get involved and refuse to let your life collect dust. Starting today.

Don't wait until you're 18 or 21 or 25...or for the weather to change, for spare time, more money, a high school diploma...now is the time to start planting.

Solomon also said that courage alone is not enough. Wisdom and discernment are part of the tightrope walk in life.

Deuteronomy 6:5-9 illustrates what all of the Bible, including Ecclesiastes, teaches about our doing. The emphasis is always on what God does and not on what his people achieve.

Deuteronomy 6:8 suggests we wear God's promises on our person. Repeat what God has done over and over again. Share it with everyone. Talk about it at home, on the road, when you go to bed, when you wake up.

Tear out this page and pray a prayer of commitment. Commit to doing something now to serve God. Nothing is too small or too big. Pray and talk about it often. Thank God for what he will achieve by using you. Thank him for what he is already doing in your life. **Tear out this page.**

Then below, design a tattoo that symbolizes what you are going to do to serve and the love from God that will help you see it through. It may be a parent no-no to get a real tat, so transfer your design to your arm or leg using markers.

Put your design all over the house as Deuteronomy suggests, as a constant reminder.

In _____ We Trust

Read Ecclesiastes 11:5-6 today.

God is faithful, God is good, he loves us beyond comprehension and asks us to trust him in the unknown, and he will do right.

It's a constant promise that will not fail. God said it, and faith is the part where you believe God is telling the truth.

I don't understand how a 90 mph Colorado wind gust takes 3 opposite ends of my backyard fence and blows them down in three different directions.

I don't really understand how heart cells know to gather together, form a heart, and start beating at the same beat in a developing fetus.

I can't understand every activity of God and all he does.

I don't know what tomorrow will bring, and you don't either. We should plant our trust in God in the morning and keep busy trusting all day long. That is Solomon's insight for us.

In removing the layers of doubt we have between us and Jesus, there are some choices. Choices your ancestors made. Choices we have to make, and choices our children will make.

One choice is to trust how God wants to use us. We may have some fear we are not able, good enough, or that we'll fail. But then comes the choice to believe what God says when he tells us "I am with you...I will help you."

Then we have to decide if we're going to say yes to what God asks.

What happens next is usually life change. Whether we said yes or no.

If yes, it doesn't mean we do it perfectly or without challenge. It does mean we become a part of what God is doing and we learn from failure.

If we decide no, we may become more stubborn, ruled by our fears, and a little more selfish. We are less a part of what God wants us to become.

Solomon tells us in Chapter 11 of his journal: Say yes. Cast your life out there, give yourself to serving others, live life regardless of the conditions.

Get into action and trust God for the results.

TRUST: assured reliance on the character, ability, strength, or truth of someone or something; hope.

Tear out this page.

Answer the questions—

Do you trust God?

Do you believe like David believed when he said, "But when I am afraid, I will put my trust in you. I praise God for what he has promised. I trust in God, so why should I be afraid? What can mere mortals do to me?" Psalm 56:3-4.

Jesus said he would never leave us or forsake us. Do you believe it?

Bury this page in a garden, in a potted plant, flower bed...as this page degrades it becomes part of the soil. We hope it becomes useful compost.

Like the buried page, we can become used by God when we say yes. Whether the plant grows or not, God is in control. We trust God to use us. Totally committed like the page which may not show results until totally used up.

If you answer no, Solomon indicates change occurs regardless. But the change looks like the farmer who waits for perfect weather and never plants. If he watches every cloud guessing at just the right one to bring rain, he will never harvest.

Just Breathe

Trusting God, for me, sometimes starts by just taking a deep breath and listening. What is it that God is telling me?

Get my brain and my ego out of the way so God has more room to work.

Removing fear, trusting God, not knowing what lies ahead, stripping layers of junk that lie between me and Jesus. Vanity, meaninglessness, emptiness, the lifeless pursuit of stuff, achievement or power...it can seem depressing and overwhelming.

All of it, though, is meant to align us with joy through God. We can engage life with joy. Remember what Solomon says especially to youth...

> "Enjoy what you have rather than desiring what you don't have. Just dreaming about nice things is meaningless" Ecclesiastes 6:9.

> "So I recommend having fun, because there is nothing better for people in this world than to eat, drink, and enjoy life. That way they will experience some happiness along with all the hard work God gives them under the sun" Ecclesiastes 8:15.

> "Young people, it's wonderful to be young! Enjoy every minute of it. Do everything you want to do; take it all in. But remember that you must give an account to God for everything you do" Ecclesiastes 11:9-10.

Tear out
this page.

Tear the page in two and use it to cover your ears
or even plug your ears (for safety, when you feel
resistance, stop.)

Spend several minutes praying today. Get in as
quiet a place as you can. Cover your ears with the
torn pages and listen. Listen to your heart beat,
your lungs fill and then empty.

The very name of God is in the breaths we take.
Try it. YAHHH (breathe in) WEHHH (breathe out).
YAHHH, WEHHH.

Listen for God to speak to you today. Ask him to
calm your mind, and work in you as you try and rid
yourself of selfish, fearful, materialistic layers
that are keeping you from really enjoying Jesus.

Listen. Read John 10:18. Rest in God's love.

cover →   listen ↑

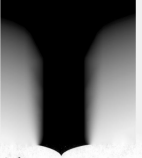

Read Ecclesiastes 11:7-8a today.
We are drawing close to the end of Solomon's journal, Ecclesiastes. With the last few pages of this devotional, we can start seeing how Solomon is resolving the questions he has raised in his investigation of life. Solomon is trying to do what this devotional has been trying to do. That is, to peel away the layers, get stripped clean of the empty and meaningless things in our lives that keep us from enjoying a passionate and sold-out relationship with Jesus.

At first look, Solomon's journal seems filled with despair and discouragement. Vanity, meaninglessness, emptiness, not finding happiness in our pursuit of stuff or achievement or power. We all die in the end.

In total it turns out this is a journal of joy. Everything to this point is showing us life without God. But now it's Solomon's observation that since we can't control what life brings—real joy and meaning lies in God's hands. If we align all we have been given with God, we can enjoy work, our families, our adventures and all that this life dishes out. Engage life.

Solomon shares that there is a sweetness and goodness to the life God has given us. We have many good things to enjoy, so enjoy it everyday. Get up in the morning and let your first words and thoughts be of thanksgiving. Thank God for the very breath you now enjoy.

If life is on hold for you, what are you waiting for?

Are you waiting until you have all the things you've always wanted? Are you waiting for a person to fulfill your life? Are you waiting until you've achieved goals or realized dreams?

Or are you, like me, starting to make the connection that waiting for life to begin is foolish. I need to engage in it now.

Life is not going to start later. It's already begun. Engage.

Tear out this page and turn it over.

Tear out the page and sleep with it tonight. When you wake up, read the verse out loud, take a deep breath, and engage life today. Don't wait.

"Always be full of joy in the Lord. I say it again—rejoice! Let everyone see that you are considerate in all you do. Remember, the Lord is coming soon.

"Don't worry about anything; instead, pray about everything. Tell God what you need, and thank him for all he has done. Then you will experience God's peace, which exceeds anything we can understand. His peace will guard your hearts and minds as you live in Christ Jesus" Philippians 4:4-7.

[Remember to Say Thank You]

Remove a layer of forgetfulness today. Remember to thank God for the life you have now. Know that your strength today comes from God and God alone. Whether it's a good day or not a good day.

Read Ecclesiastes 11:7-8 today.

Noviana Malewa is a teen living in Indonesia. She lives a life not much different from any other teen in the world struggling with similar teen issues—with one exception.

Life presented a traumatic and dark day that left a permanent reminder on Noviana's face.

Voice of the Martyrs is a nonprofit interdenominational ministry that works worldwide to help Christians who are persecuted for their faith.

They reported that on October 29, 2005, Noviana and three of her friends were walking on a school path when they were assaulted by Islamic jihadists with machetes. Noviana survived but suffered a deep slash across her face and neck.

Her friends were decapitated.

If that was not horrible enough, Noviana's attackers vowed to hunt her down and kill her and other teenage Christians, remove their heads, and leave them on the steps of the church as a present.

Solomon suggests we enjoy life now and for however many years we may have. Remember, though, that this life does not present its joy easily. Fundamentally it is unreliable. There will be days, maybe many days of pain and darkness.

So how do you find joy in the midst of that? How does Noviana find joy?

The same way Paul did. Remembering in the darkest of days we still have a loving Father who is present in all of it and we lean on his sufficiency.

(wnd.com/news/article.asp?ARTICLE_ID=53450)

"**I** know how to live on almost nothing or with everything. **I** have learned the secret of living in every situation, whether it is with a full stomach or empty, with plenty or little. For **I** can do everything through Christ, who gives me strength" Philippians 4:12-13.

This kind of contentment is learned Paul says. Solomon says "remember"—indicating a choice. Choose to reflect on who God is, then engage life with contentment.

What gave Paul endurance? What relieved the tension and allowed him to be so relaxed inside? Doing everything through Christ requires conviction. Believing that Jesus is pouring his power into us every day.

When we believe this truth as Noviana believes this—nothing is out of control. We can truly do everything God asks us to do with the help of Jesus, who gives us the strength and power.

Tear out the page and draw on it, put color on it. Then design and roll it into a bracelet or a ring or an earring or an ankle bracelet or a tie, something you can wear today.

Don't eat today and wear your page as a reminder to pray and know you can do everything through Christ, who gives you strength in every situation.

Repeat the verse often today.

Tear out this page.
Turn it over.
Photograph it with your cell phone and make it a display on your phone.
Every time you use your phone today and view your display, be reminded to enjoy every single minute of your youth.
Live openly and rightly before God, who wants us to enjoy life. his way.

"Young people, it's wonderful to be young! Enjoy every minute of it. Do everything you want to do; take it all in. But remember that you must give an account to God for everything you do."

Ecclesiastes 11:9

Joy Stealers

You've been tearing away page after page, stripping away the layers between you and Jesus. You may have even started looking at your life differently and looking at the things you pursue differently. You may even be inspired to live life with a new gusto and immediacy.

And then comes along one circumstance, one person, one misdirected purpose, one worry, one anxiety, and all the joy vanishes.

Read Ecclesiastes 11:10 today.

It's a challenging word picture Solomon paints for us, and there is no simple or magical formula that can take us from depression to joy. But there is a process. Solomon's picture involves our will and our desire and our singleness of mind.

There are small layers of anxiety, worry, difficulties, irritations, and responsibilities that build up and can create a much larger layer. A layer that can lead to wishing things were different, that leads us to become cynical or resentful toward God. They are the joy-stealer layers.

Solomon suggests we protect our heart from the stealers.

Worrying about tomorrow—a tomorrow you can't control anyway.

Trying to please other people—it's a weak and pointless pursuit.

Becoming angry at God and blaming him for what is happening to us.

Solomon's first insight to dealing with this is to deal with our heart and consciously remove the attitude of anxiety. Stake your attitude to the ground, walk away, and don't go back to that place. Leave it for God to deal with. Because, as Solomon has pointed out many times, we can't change the things we can't change.

When I feel the frustration and the anxiety building up, I can choose to take God's hand and decide to get rid of the "might have beens" and the "what ifs" that keep piling up in my mind. I can choose to leave behind anxiety and worry and live life today in the presence of a loving God.

Then there is the outer part of life to deal with. Solomon has never suggested we don't change the things we can in our life. He has pointed out many times in his journal that we have to walk through the troubles in this life. If there is a barrier you can remove, by all means, remove it. But difficulty will invade our joy. It's part of the journey.

There is another choice to be made. You and I can both avoid the sin that causes pain. Solomon suggests over and over to avoid foolishness and foolish living. But still life brings trouble.

Walk through it. Solomon has. And he knows that the trouble has a purpose in it, and that purpose is from God who promised to work it out for our good.

This is a very hard thing to do.

Tear out this page.

Draw something, write something, glue something on the page that represents something causing you pain or worry or anxiety or maybe resentment toward God.

As you pray today, make a choice. Choose to walk through this moment and trust that God has a purpose and that he will work things together for your good.

Then go outside and stake this page to the ground with something. Leave it there and walk away. Leave it with God.

Prodding Wisdom

"The words of the wise are like cattle prods—painful but helpful" Ecclesiastes 12:11. Ouch and thank you. May I have another?

Read Ecclesiastes 12:1-2 today.

This devotional is almost out of pages and Solomon is about to conclude his journal, but not without some parting thoughts.

Solomon's conclusion should not come as a surprise if you started this devotional from the front and worked your way to the end.

The fullness of life, enjoyment of life, contentment in life can't be found apart from lining up our lives with God.

The one certain fact about our existence Solomon has told us is that someday we'll die, and it will be a waste of life if you live it and never discover why you are here. Learn the secret of true existence before you die.

Solomon concludes by addressing youth again—Remember your Creator.

Not forgetting suggests, yet again, a decision. Decide in your heart to draw near and trust God. It is also being suggested that you do it before it's too late. Before you conclude that there is no hope in this life.

If we commit ourselves to God and leave the self-sufficient habits behind, it is there we'll find meaning.

Let this be your prayer today—

Dear God, you created every fiber of my being. You knew me before I was even in my mother's womb. You also know what is best for me, so I will revolve my life around your plan. I am ready to do life your way.

When you and I remember God by committing our lives to his plan no matter what our age, we can find the meaning of life and what existence is all about.

If we choose to go through life searching for meaning in our stuff, our pleasure, our achievements—if we stick with "it's all about me" and demand control that we can't have, we may just die repeating these words from Solomon...

"EVERYTHING IS MEANINGLESS," SAYS THE TEACHER, "COMPLETELY MEANINGLESS."

Solomon's words are intended to impact us more than just any book. The words are meant to penetrate and plant truth in our minds and hearts. Right into the very core of our being. Solomon wrote the words, but they come from the heart of God.

Solomon's journal prods us like sheep to a better place, a safer place, a more joyful and fulfilling place. The word pictures break through selfishness and help strip our lives clean of meaningless pursuits and replace them with the most valuable gift of all and the meaning of it all—a passionate relationship with Jesus and a life filled with and directed by God.

Are you being prodded by God? Where do you think he is leading you?

What do you pray will change in your life as you get "stripped clean"?

If Jesus were to eat dinner with you tonight, what would you two talk about?

Tear out this page.

Read the verse out loud before you go to sleep tonight. Then put this page inside your pillowcase or under whatever you lay your head on at night.

Pray for God to penetrate your heart with his Word even as you sleep.

"And I am convinced that nothing can ever separate us from God's love. Neither death nor life, neither angels nor demons, neither our fears for today nor our worries about tomorrow—not even the powers of hell can separate us from God's love. No power in the sky above or in the earth below—indeed, nothing in all creation will ever be able to separate us from the love of God that is revealed in Christ Jesus our Lord" Romans 8:38-39.

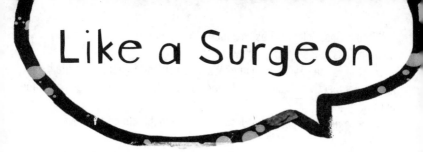

Like a Surgeon

Read Ecclesiastes 12:9-12 today.

God designed us to be empty without him, and Solomon has weaved this truth between every line of his journal. He has said it in many ways with many different word pictures.

Solomon has searched and investigated and tested and experienced life without God and wants us to hear it clearly and carefully.

Like the surgeon who has done the surgery before, been a part of the research into the surgery, has the intellect and the skill to perform the surgery, knows what he is talking about, and implores you to listen as he evaluates your condition.

Solomon has been through it all and been a skeptic and cynic and even a rebel. He implores that we please listen. His evaluation has been careful and thorough. He has probed and tested and weighed and searched out and arranged his ideas for us, in an orderly fashion. They are upright, true, honest, and sincere. Please listen...this is truth.

Solomon's wisdom is credible and he tells the truth about life. Why would we not listen?

Listen, the summary is this: God has designed you and me to be empty without him. In the beginning what God made was good, and we were designed to find happiness and contentment first in the Creator then in creation.

It's a constant struggle to get stripped clean and be filled with God, and I still fall into a pursuit of stuff that does not satisfy. Solomon's question at the very beginning of his journal rings in my ears—What do people get for all their hard work under the sun?

Under the sun, without God, all of my selfish pursuits gain nothing of eternal value.

Without God, Solomon has concluded time and time again, it is meaningless, chasing after the wind.

So what is the pay off for living? What do you and I gain in this life if we keep a perspective of God in our lives? I believe Solomon would answer, "You get God."

We become God's poem and Jesus' friend, lavished in perfect love.

Tear a hole in the middle of the page.

Tear out this page.

Then tear a hole in the middle of the page. Stick your hand through the hole.

As the page hangs from your wrist, spend some time praying. Thank God for filling the emptiness he designed us with. Let go of those things that Solomon concluded are meaningless and won't fill that space inside.

When you finish praying, tape the page to a window. As the morning sunlight shines through the hole you tore in the page, let it be a reminder to fill your life with Jesus each and every morning.

The End Is the Beginning

Read Ecclesiastes 12:13-14 today.

This is the last page of this devotional, and it is the end of Solomon's journal. Fear God and obey his commands, for this is everyone's duty.

Becoming a whole person, "stripped clean" of the layers that lead to emptiness, hangs on the words *fear God*.

Not running from God, seeing him as a threat or terror. Rather it's honor, reverence, and awe.

Fear that starts with faith and ends in response.

Faith in his existence—all of creation cries his name.

Experience grace. When we admit our corruption and sin and lay it before God, that is fear, and when we receive forgiveness, that is grace.

Awe. Total amazement and thankfulness for his wisdom and creation. How incredible and unsearchable is the knowledge of God.

Respond. There is a way to fill that emptiness that God designed into us. There is hope and transformation. There is help in our constant effort to be "stripped clean."

Choice.

Solomon reveals in the last verse of Ecclesiastes that we will all be stripped bare and we will be seen as we are. It is a reminder that no part of our lives is hidden from God. Nothing.

That's were grace comes in. It was the way God made things right. God did what we could not do. He placed all judgement on his son Jesus for everything we have and will do wrong. Jesus took it on, and suffered. For us.

Jesus was stripped clean of everything for us. He was stripped of his clothes, his dignity, his blood, his Father's presence, and his life. Stripped of everything so we could have a choice.

This devotional has been an active illustration of stripping away things that keep us from a passionate relationship with Jesus, materialism...and more. We've stripped everything away, down to the Cross. How will you respond?

Tear out this page.

Tear off the front and back covers. Send me the front cover with your prayer requests, and let me know what you're doing to get stripped clean. Tear off the back cover and do what it says on it.

Use the wire that's left to sculpt a cross. Find a quiet place where you can read the verse below out loud and then pray. I'm not going to tell you what to pray for or how to pray. You've stripped away a lot between you and Jesus, and now is the time to lay it all down at his feet. Respond to Jesus' call—follow me. In Jesus you're not loved any more or any less than he loves you right now.

After you read the verse, speak or write down your response to Jesus. Then burn this page. Let it be the last reminder that in Jesus we are new. The old is gone and the new life has come.

"This means that anyone who belongs to Christ has become a new person. the old life is gone; a new life has begun!

"And all of this is a gift from God, who brought us back to himself through Christ. And God has given us this task of reconciling people to him. For God was in Christ, reconciling the world to himself, no longer counting people's sins against them. And he gave us this wonderful message of reconciliation. So we are Christ's ambassadors; God is making his appeal through us. We speak for Christ when we plead, Come back to God!" 2 Corinthians 5:17-20.